Vanisher

Vanisher

Matthew Petchinsky

1

Vanisher: How to Disappear from the Internet Without Losing Your Life

BY: Matthew Petchinsky

Disclaimer

This book, *Vanisher: How to Disappear from the Internet Without Losing Your Life*, is provided for **educational and informational purposes only.** It is not intended as legal advice, financial advice, or a substitute for professional consultation in law, cybersecurity, or digital forensics. Readers are strongly encouraged to seek qualified professional guidance before making decisions that could affect their legal, financial, or personal standing.

The author and publisher explicitly state:

1. **No Liability for Misuse**
   The strategies, methods, and tools described in this book are intended to empower individuals to protect their privacy, manage their digital footprint, and reclaim personal sovereignty in an age of mass data collection. They are not intended to support, encourage, or enable illegal activity. The author and publisher disclaim any and all responsibility for readers who misuse, misapply, or abuse this information for unlawful purposes. By using this book, you agree that neither the author nor the publisher can be held liable for consequences resulting from your actions.

2.Educational Intent Only

The material herein is designed to raise awareness about digital surveillance, privacy erosion, and the practical steps individuals may take to safeguard themselves. It is not written as a manual for criminal behavior, fraud, or evasion of legitimate legal obligations.

3.Evolving Technology Warning

The landscape of digital privacy, cybersecurity, and surveillance changes rapidly. What may be effective today may become obsolete, counterproductive, or even risky in the future. The author and publisher make no guarantees that the platforms, tools, or services discussed will remain operational, safe, or effective. Readers are responsible for verifying the current reliability, legality, and ethical appropriateness of any resource before use.

4.Jurisdictional Differences

Privacy rights, data protection laws, and digital freedoms vary across jurisdictions. What is legal in one country may be restricted or unlawful in another. Readers are responsible for understanding and complying with the laws of their own country or region.

4.Ethical Use Statement

The spirit of this book is one of empowerment, sovereignty, and protection — not harm. Readers are urged to apply these lessons ethically, to safeguard themselves and others, and to recognize the distinction between privacy and deception.

5.No Absolute Guarantee

While the methods described can significantly reduce exposure, there is no way to guarantee complete anonymity or permanent disappearance. Any digital system can be compromised. Use of the information in this book should be accompanied by common sense, discretion, and caution.

6.Personal Responsibility

By reading and applying concepts from this book, you acknowledge that your choices and actions are your responsibility alone. Digital disappearance is a personal journey, and you assume full accountability for any outcomes that result from applying the techniques herein.

Closing Note

This book exists to illuminate, to teach, and to equip you with awareness in a world where surveillance is the norm. The author and publisher encourage you to use this knowledge to strengthen your resilience, defend your sovereignty, and cultivate a life of dignity and freedom. Above all, use it wisely, use it ethically, and use it with caution.

Introduction

The Quiet Theft of Power

Every time you open an app, swipe your card, or even pause to look at an ad, you leave behind a trail. These fragments of your life—where you go, what you buy, who you talk to, what you think about—are harvested, packaged, and sold. It's a surveillance economy, and its favorite product is you.

The danger isn't just that companies know too much. It's that control slips quietly out of your hands. Algorithms decide what news you see, whether you get approved for a loan, or even how much you'll pay for a flight. Governments and corporations collaborate in building vast archives of your behavior. And worse still—this information becomes a weapon when it falls into the wrong hands: hackers, stalkers, abusive partners, or employers who decide you're no longer worth the risk.

The Illusion of Connection

The internet promised freedom, but it delivered dependence. Most people now live in a glass house they can't escape. Social media became the passport to belonging. Email addresses became the price of entry into jobs, banking, and even grocery stores. Every layer of convenience tied us more tightly into a system designed not for our empowerment, but for our exploitation.

And then came the age of cancellation, where one mistake—or one targeted smear—can wipe out your reputation, your career, even your sense of safety. Suddenly, the ability to vanish, to step outside the network of constant scrutiny, is no longer paranoia. It's survival.

The Blueprint to Vanish and Thrive

This book is not about fear. It is about freedom. It is not about abandoning your life, but about reclaiming it. You will learn how to surgically erase your digital footprint, cancel-proof your identity, and design a personal strategy that allows you to exist on your terms.

Inside, you'll find practical systems—step-by-step methods to:

- Scrub yourself from data brokers and search engines.
- Use stealth technologies that protect your everyday communications.
- Set up financial systems that preserve anonymity without sacrificing opportunity.
- Master the art of a controlled online identity: one that shields, protects, and empowers instead of exposing.
- Build resilience against employers, corporations, and anyone who believes they own your information.

This is not about running from life—it is about living more fully within it. Once you understand how surveillance steals your power, you'll see why disappearing is not an escape but an evolution.

By the time you finish, you'll hold the keys to sovereignty in the digital age. You'll become invisible to the systems designed to trap you—and visible only where *you* choose to shine.

Welcome to the art of vanishing. Welcome to *Vanisher*.

Chapter 1: The Data You Forgot You Gave

The Invisible Exchange

Most people think about data leaks as rare events—massive hacks splashed across the news, credit card numbers stolen in bulk, or a celebrity's private messages exposed. But the truth is far more unsettling: you've been giving away your data every day, often without realizing it.

Every online form, loyalty program, free app, or "agree to terms" button was a silent contract. You gave away a piece of yourself, usually in exchange for something that seemed harmless—ten percent off a purchase, a free trial, or faster checkout. The internet made this bargain so routine that you barely notice it anymore. But those fragments of information didn't stay where you left them. They multiplied. They spread. They became part of an ecosystem designed to know you better than you know yourself.

The Bread Crumbs That Built Your Shadow

Let's examine just how much you've already given away:

- **Your Name and Contact Info**: Every newsletter signup, every delivery order, every online account added another entry into data broker archives.
- **Your Location**: Apps and websites ask for "location permissions," sometimes even when they don't need them. Combined with GPS pings, Wi-Fi logins, and shipping addresses, your movements are mapped in frightening detail.
- **Your Habits and Preferences**: Think of the quizzes, polls, and games that promised to "reveal your personality type" or "which character you are." Each click filled in another blank in your behavioral profile.
- **Your Financial Footprint**: Online purchases, banking apps, ride-hailing services, food delivery, and digital wallets create transaction trails that can be cross-referenced for spending habits, income level, and even debt risk.
- **Your Conversations**: Messaging apps, smart speakers, and even email subject lines are parsed for keywords. That's not science fiction—it's routine marketing practice.
- **Your Biometrics**: Face scans to unlock your phone, voice commands to virtual assistants, and even step counters on fitness apps—all contribute to a database of your physical identity.

On their own, none of these things may seem dangerous. But stitched together, they create what's called a **digital shadow**—a living replica of you that exists inside corporate servers. This version of you can be bought, sold, scored, and judged without your knowledge or consent.

The Power of Forgotten Data

The most dangerous data isn't what you remember giving—it's what you've forgotten. That Yahoo email account you abandoned in 2009? Still active in data leaks. That MySpace profile you never deleted? Still indexed by certain archives. That free weather app you downloaded once and never used again? Still feeding location data to third-party advertisers.

Data doesn't die when you stop paying attention. It lingers. It duplicates. In many cases, it grows more valuable over time, because historical records provide context for predicting your future behavior. To a surveillance system, the version of you from ten years ago is just as useful as the version of you today—because together they show a pattern.

The Illusion of Harmlessness

Here's how the trap works:

- The app looks free.
- The form looks routine.
- The "yes" button looks harmless.

But every digital service is designed with one hidden truth: if you aren't paying for the product, *you are the product.*

Consider a single Instagram photo. On the surface, it's just an image you shared with friends. But under the hood, it contains:

- Metadata about the time and location of capture.
- Facial recognition points mapped to your features.
- Information about the device you used.
- Tags, comments, and likes that signal your interests and network.

What looked like a moment of self-expression became a goldmine of machine-readable signals. Now multiply that by every post you've ever made, across every platform. That's not harmless—that's the scaffolding of your surveillance profile.

Why You Forgot

Surveillance thrives on invisibility. The reason you've forgotten the data you gave is because you were *meant* to forget. The agreements are hidden in walls of legalese. The permissions are buried in default settings. The platforms are engineered to make it effortless to say "yes" and exhausting to say "no."

Psychologists call this **consent fatigue**—when the endless barrage of pop-ups and permissions dulls your ability to pay attention. You click "allow" or "accept" just to make the screen go away. And with each tiny surrender, you handed over a piece of your life.

The Consequences of Accumulated Trust

Your forgotten data can be used against you in ways you never imagined:

- **Price Discrimination**: Airlines and retailers adjust prices based on your browsing history, location, and device type.
- **Job Applications**: Employers now use reputation scoring tools that scrape your old posts, even the ones you thought were deleted.
- **Legal Risks**: Lawsuits and investigations sometimes unearth decade-old emails or posts to attack credibility.
- **Identity Theft**: Criminals exploit old, unsecured accounts to pivot into your newer, more important ones.

The quiet accumulation of forgotten data creates a situation where you're judged not by who you are today, but by the traces you left behind.

The First Step to Vanishing

Before you can reclaim your sovereignty, you must confront a simple truth: you've been leaving fingerprints everywhere, and most of them you no longer remember.

This chapter is not about shame. It is about awareness. The forgotten data you left behind is not a sign of failure—it is evidence of how skillfully the system was built to capture you.

The first step to vanishing is to **catalogue your shadow.**

Chapter 2: Self-Destruct Your Digital Doppelgänger

The Birth of Your Doppelgänger

By now, you understand that every trace you've ever left online has been collected, copied, and stitched together into a shadow version of yourself — your **digital doppelgänger.**

It is not flesh and bone, but algorithms and metadata. It doesn't age the way you do, but it grows every time you post, purchase, swipe, or search. It knows your past addresses, your old phone numbers, your favorite brands, and your late-night obsessions. In some ways, it knows you better than you know yourself, because it remembers everything you've forgotten.

But here's the terrifying truth: this doppelgänger does not serve you. It serves the system.

- To advertisers, it's a profile that can be manipulated into spending.
- To employers, it's a dossier that can determine whether you're hired.
- To governments, it's a risk assessment that dictates your freedoms.
- To criminals, it's a treasure chest waiting to be broken open.

Your digital twin walks ahead of you into every room, whispering your secrets to those who profit from them.

Why It Must Die

The goal of this book is not just to protect your privacy — it is to free you from the chains of surveillance. And that means your doppelgänger has to be destroyed.

If you don't dismantle it, you will always be playing defense. You will always be subject to manipulation, judgment, and exploitation. Your digital doppelgänger will live on long after you're gone, influencing how your children, your business, or your legacy is treated.

To vanish is not to run away — it is to **self-destruct strategically.** It is to strip power away from this artificial you and reclaim it for your living, breathing self.

The Tools of Self-Destruction

Destroying your digital doppelgänger doesn't happen with one click. There is no "delete all" button. Instead, you must think like a saboteur dismantling an enemy fortress:

1. **Identify the structures that keep it alive.**
2. **Pull the plugs that feed it.**
3. **Replace its presence with controlled decoys.**

Let's break these down.

1. Identify the Structures

Your digital doppelgänger is housed in databases. Some are obvious — Facebook, Google, Amazon. Others are hidden — data brokers, background check services, advertising exchanges, dark web dumps. These structures are like organs, each pumping life into the larger body of your digital twin. You must map them before you can dismantle them.

2. Pull the Plugs

Once you know where your doppelgänger lives, you begin the self-destruction process. This involves:

- **Deletions:** Removing old accounts, photos, posts, and files.
- **Obfuscations:** Replacing real information with fake entries to poison the dataset.
- **Opt-outs:** Forcing data brokers to purge or suppress your records.
- **Permission Revocations:** Denying apps and platforms access to collect more.

The point is not to reach zero data — that's impossible. The point is to starve the doppelgänger until it's weak, fragmented, and unreliable.

3. Replace With Controlled Decoys

Total invisibility raises suspicion in the digital world. Employers, banks, and even friends expect some kind of online footprint. That's why part of the art of vanishing is **strategic misdirection.**

You create a controlled, minimalist identity — a simple professional profile, a single email account, a handful of harmless interests — that feeds the system just enough to appear functional. Meanwhile, your real self lives behind layers of protection.

This decoy becomes the ghost-mask you wear online while your true movements remain hidden.

The Psychology of Erasure

Self-destructing your digital doppelgänger is not just technical — it's psychological. The system has conditioned you to believe you need it. That without constant posting, liking, and sharing, you don't exist.

But ask yourself: *Who are you without the feed? Who are you without the algorithm?*

Erasing your doppelgänger forces you to re-learn sovereignty. It is uncomfortable at first, even frightening, because silence feels like absence. But gradually, you discover that what you deleted was never you at all — it was an imitation designed to be consumed.

What "Death" Looks Like

When your digital doppelgänger begins to crumble, you'll notice changes:

- Ads become less targeted, more generic.
- Background checks return less detail.
- Search engines struggle to tie your name to activity.
- The endless flood of spam and calls begins to slow.

To the system, you will appear unreliable, incomplete, a ghost slipping through cracks. That's the signal that you've weakened your doppelgänger enough to live without it.

The Mission Ahead

This chapter has given you the strategy and mindset: know the doppelgänger, starve it, and replace it with a decoy.

You are not powerless. You built this shadow over years of invisible consent. Now, with awareness and action, you will dismantle it piece by piece — until the only version of you that exists is the one you choose.

Chapter 3: Strike the First Blows — Your Digital Vanishing Checklist

Your digital doppelgänger thrives on forgotten accounts, unguarded profiles, and shadow records you didn't know existed. The fastest way to weaken it is to **audit, delete, and disrupt.** This chapter hands you a systematic checklist to begin the process. Think of it as a demolition guide: we'll start with the surface-level cracks before moving into the foundations that hold your doppelgänger together.

Phase One: The Easy Wins

These are the low-hanging fruit — actions you can take immediately to begin reclaiming control.

1. **Old Email Accounts**
    - Search your memory for past providers: Yahoo, Hotmail, AOL, Outlook, etc.
    - Log in if possible. If you can't, request account recovery.
    - Delete accounts entirely, or if that's not possible, strip them of personal data.
2. **Forgotten Social Media Profiles**
    - MySpace, Friendster, Vine, Google+, LiveJournal, Tumblr.
    - Use a people search tool (Spokeo, Pipl, PeekYou) to see what still surfaces under your name.
    - Deactivate or delete what you find.
3. **Retail Loyalty Programs**
    - Old grocery cards, bookstore memberships, coffee rewards apps.
    - Cancel or request data deletion through customer service.
4. **Email Subscriptions**
    - Use a service like Unroll.me or simply search your inbox for "unsubscribe."
    - Remove as many as possible — each list is another database holding your info.

Phase Two: The Hidden Reservoirs

Now we dig into less obvious places where your data hides.

1. **Data Brokers**
    - Search for your name on common brokers: Whitepages, Spokeo, Intelius, BeenVerified, PeopleFinders, etc.
    - Use opt-out guides (many are published by privacy activists) to request removal.
    - Bookmark a calendar reminder: brokers repopulate; you may need to repeat every 6–12 months.
2. **Search Engines**
    - Google yourself. Bing yourself. Don't stop at page one — dig deep.
    - For sensitive links, use Google's "Remove Outdated Content" tool.
    - If content is hosted on a site you don't control, contact the webmaster with a removal request.
3. **Cloud Storage & Forgotten Apps**
    - Check old Dropbox, iCloud, OneDrive, Google Drive accounts.
    - Delete anything sensitive. Close the account if unused.
    - Review app permissions on your current devices and revoke unnecessary ones.
4. **Public Records**
    - Property deeds, voter registrations, marriage/divorce records often appear online.
    - Where legal, request redaction of personal details (some states offer this for safety reasons).

Phase Three: Advanced Disruption

Here's where you start sabotaging the very structure of your digital doppelgänger.

1. **Poison the Data Wells**
    - Where deletion isn't possible, feed misleading data: change birth dates, nicknames, old addresses.
    - Create junk accounts that misdirect ad trackers (example: a decoy shopping profile with fake preferences).
2. **Scrub Metadata**

- Photos carry EXIF data (time, location, device type). Before sharing, strip metadata using tools like ExifTool or built-in "remove info" settings.
- Delete old uploads from forums or file-sharing platforms where metadata can still live.

3.Phone & Device Trails

- Turn off "location history" on Google, Apple, Facebook.
- Purge saved Wi-Fi networks from devices (these logs can be mined).
- Reset advertising IDs on iOS and Android.

4.Financial Shadows

- Audit every digital wallet, PayPal, Venmo, CashApp, and online banking account.
- Delete transaction history where possible.
- Consider a privacy-first bank or credit union for future transactions.

5.Search for Your Doppelgänger

- Use "Have I Been Pwned" to find breached accounts tied to your emails.
- Use services like DeleteMe or Kanary (paid, but effective) to automate removals.
- Maintain a spreadsheet logging every account, broker, and request — your erasure campaign needs a map.

Phase Four: The Decoy Identity

Remember: you don't want to vanish completely. A ghost raises suspicion. A decoy keeps you safe.

1. **Build a Minimal Professional Presence**

- Keep a LinkedIn with sanitized details (no birthday, no personal phone).
- Maintain one clean email for legitimate services (banking, government, professional).

2.Establish Your Mask

- Create harmless interests for ad networks to latch onto (e.g., gardening, classic films).
- Ensure this "digital mask" reflects nothing sensitive but still satisfies systems that expect a user profile.

Maintaining the Strike

Self-destruction isn't a one-time act — it's ongoing warfare. Once you've completed your first sweep:

- **Repeat every six months.**
- **Document everything.** The act of keeping a log prevents forgotten accounts from resurfacing.
- **Stay vigilant.** New brokers and leaks appear constantly.

The First Blows Landed

By completing this checklist, you've already weakened your doppelgänger. Ads will begin to lose precision. Searches will start returning less detail. Data brokers will grow frustrated with outdated, incomplete records.

You won't be invisible yet, but you'll feel the shift: the machine no longer knows you as well as it once did.

Chapter 4: The Stealth Arsenal — Tools for Digital Disappearance

When you dismantle your digital doppelgänger, you create a void. The system will immediately try to refill that void with new data. If you continue browsing, messaging, and transacting as usual, the shadow will rebuild itself — stronger, faster, and smarter than before.

The solution is to **replace exposure with stealth.** This chapter is your weapons locker: the practical tools that keep you invisible while still allowing you to function in a hyperconnected world.

1. VPNs — Cloaking Your Location and Traffic

A **Virtual Private Network (VPN)** creates a secure tunnel between you and the internet. Without one, every site you visit knows your IP address — essentially your digital home address. With a VPN, you can appear to be browsing from anywhere in the world.

What to Look For in a VPN:

- **No-logs policy:** Ensures the provider isn't storing your activity.
- **Independent audits:** Proof that their claims are tested by third parties.
- **Kill switch:** Cuts your connection if the VPN drops, preventing leaks.
- **Multi-hop routing:** Some VPNs let you pass traffic through two countries for extra cover.

Top Recommendations:

- ProtonVPN (privacy-first, Swiss-based).
- Mullvad (anonymous sign-up with cash or crypto).
- IVPN (transparent policies, strong ethics).

Pro Tip: Rotate server locations regularly. Don't just pick one country and stick to it — that creates a predictable pattern.

2. Browsers — The Gatekeepers of Your Activity

Your browser is one of the leakiest tools in your digital life. Cookies, trackers, fingerprinting scripts — all of these are designed to rebuild your identity in seconds.

Stealth Browsers to Use:

- **Brave:** Chromium-based, blocks trackers by default, integrates with Tor.
- **Firefox with Extensions:** Add-ons like uBlock Origin, Privacy Badger, and NoScript make it a fortress.
- **Tor Browser:** Routes traffic through multiple encrypted relays. Slower, but unmatched for anonymity.

Settings Checklist:

- Disable third-party cookies.
- Turn off "save passwords."
- Clear cache on exit.
- Use container tabs (Firefox) or profiles to silo identities.

Pro Tip: Separate browsing into categories. For example, one browser for professional/financial accounts (your decoy identity), another for private searching, and Tor for anything truly sensitive. Never cross the streams.

3. Encrypted Messaging — Silent Channels

Your text messages and standard emails are postcards in the digital world — anyone can read them. Encrypted messaging ensures only you and the intended recipient can see the content.

Best-in-Class Tools:

- **Signal:** Open-source, end-to-end encryption, disappearing messages, minimal metadata.
- **Session:** Decentralized, doesn't require a phone number.
- **ProtonMail / Tutanota:** Encrypted email providers based in strong privacy jurisdictions.

What to Avoid:

- SMS texting — inherently insecure.
- WhatsApp — encrypted, but owned by Meta (data mining is inevitable).
- Gmail — convenient, but Google scans and monetizes data.

Pro Tip: Set default timers for disappearing messages. The less stored, the less exposed.

4. Fake Identities — The Art of the Decoy

Total erasure makes you suspicious. That's why a **fake but functional identity** is part of the stealth toolkit. This decoy satisfies systems that expect data while shielding your real self.

Building a Decoy Identity:

- Use alias generators (like Fakenamegenerator.com) for names, birthdays, and addresses.
- Create a decoy email via ProtonMail, Tutanota, or even a "throwaway" Gmail.
- Set up a burner social media profile with harmless content (cats, books, travel).

Rules for Decoy Management:

- Keep it consistent: never cross wires with your real details.
- Feed it just enough to look real (one or two posts a month).
- Never use the decoy for banking, government, or legal documents.

Pro Tip: Think of your decoy as a mask you wear at a party — convincing enough to blend in, but never confused with the real you.

5. Burner Phones — Disappearing Devices

Your smartphone is a surveillance beacon — GPS, microphone, accelerometer, and constant pings to towers. A **burner phone** is your disposable shield.

When to Use a Burner:

- Signing up for services requiring a phone number.
- Communicating in high-risk situations.
- Travel where you don't want your primary device tracked.

Options:

- Buy prepaid phones with cash at big-box stores.
- Use secondary SIM cards (when possible).
- Consider eSIM apps like Hushed or MySudo for temporary numbers.

Rules for Burners:

- Never log into your main accounts on a burner.
- Never carry your real and burner phone together — location triangulation can link them.
- Use burners sparingly and discard when compromised.

6. Passwords and Authentication — Locking the Gates

Your stealth identity is only as strong as its weakest password.

- Use a password manager (Bitwarden, KeePassXC, 1Password).
- Generate 20+ character unique strings for every account.
- Enable 2FA (two-factor authentication) with authenticator apps, **not** SMS codes.

Pro Tip: For critical accounts, use hardware keys (YubiKey or SoloKey). These are nearly impossible to phish.

7. Layering Stealth — Defense in Depth

No single tool makes you vanish. True stealth comes from **layering:**

- VPN + Tor for browsing.
- Decoy accounts for surface presence.
- Signal for conversations.
- Burner numbers for sign-ups.
- Password managers for compartmentalization.

Each layer adds friction for anyone trying to rebuild your doppelgänger. Think of it as stacking shields — if one breaks, the others still hold.

The Mindset of Stealth

Tools alone won't save you. Stealth is a discipline:

- Always assume you're being watched.
- Treat convenience as a red flag — the easier it is, the more it costs in privacy.
- Never reuse an identity — once linked, it's burned.

The tools in this chapter are your armor, but your mindset is the sword. To thrive in stealth, you must be patient, consistent, and deliberate.

What Comes Next

You've struck the first blows and armed yourself with the right tools. But stealth is not just about surviving — it's about thriving.

Because disappearing doesn't mean giving up your life. It means reclaiming it.

Chapter 5: Financial Stealth — Money That Moves in Shadows

Money is the bloodstream of your digital doppelgänger. Every card swipe, online order, or mobile transfer leaves behind a trail that corporations and governments mine relentlessly. If you want to vanish, you must learn how to move money without leaving a glowing signature behind.

This isn't about illegal activity. It's about **strategic privacy.** Financial stealth means designing systems where your spending, saving, and earning work for you — not against you.

1. The Surveillance Economy of Money

Before you build stealth, you need to understand how the system watches you:

- **Credit & Debit Cards:** Every purchase is logged by banks, shared with credit bureaus, and sometimes sold to marketers.
- **Online Payment Platforms:** PayPal, Venmo, CashApp — all track transactions, contacts, and behavioral data.
- **Bank Accounts:** Most traditional banks monitor for "suspicious activity," which can be as simple as withdrawing cash in unusual amounts.
- **Subscription Services:** Netflix, Spotify, Amazon — they don't just charge you; they build profiles on your habits.

The result? A financial paper trail so detailed it can reconstruct your life in near real-time.

2. Cash — The Original Stealth Currency

Cash is still king when it comes to anonymity. It leaves no digital record, and its use creates natural breaks in your doppelgänger's profile.

Cash Strategies:

- Pay in cash whenever possible for day-to-day expenses (groceries, dining, gas).
- Keep emergency reserves hidden in safe locations — cash doesn't go offline.
- Use cash to fund prepaid debit cards when electronic payment is unavoidable.

Pro Tip: Rotate your withdrawal locations and amounts. Withdrawing the same amount from the same ATM creates patterns banks can track.

3. Privacy-First Banking

If you need a bank, choose one that respects privacy. Large institutions like Wells Fargo or Chase are deeply embedded in the surveillance economy. Smaller, independent banks and credit unions often have fewer data-sharing agreements.

Checklist for Choosing a Bank:

- Avoid banks tied to major credit card issuers (Visa, Mastercard loyalty tracking).
- Favor credit unions — member-owned, less incentive to sell data.
- Ask directly about their data-sharing policies.

Pro Tip: Keep accounts compartmentalized — one account for necessary bills, another for savings, another for decoy transactions.

4. Prepaid & Anonymous Cards

Prepaid debit cards are powerful stealth tools when used correctly. They can be purchased with cash, funded discreetly, and used online without linking to your identity.

Rules for Prepaid Stealth:

- Always buy cards in-store with cash, not online.
- Register with decoy details if required.
- Never tie a prepaid card to your main phone number or address.

Some countries even offer "gift" debit cards usable internationally — ideal for keeping small sums outside surveillance grids.

5. Cryptocurrency — The Double-Edged Sword

Crypto is both a shield and a trap. While it offers privacy in theory, most people use it in ways that make them more traceable than cash.

Stealth-Friendly Coins:

- **Monero (XMR):** Designed for privacy, with ring signatures and stealth addresses.
- **Zcash (ZEC):** Offers shielded transactions (though optional).
- **Bitcoin (BTC):** Transparent by default — use only with mixing services or privacy wallets.

Safe Crypto Practices:

- Never buy directly from exchanges that require full ID (like Coinbase). Use peer-to-peer marketplaces instead.
- Always move coins through a personal wallet before spending or trading.
- Use VPNs and Tor to hide IP addresses when transacting.
- Consider "mixers" or privacy protocols that obscure transaction trails.

Warning: Most crypto is traceable when linked to your real identity. Treat it as semi-anonymous, not invisible.

6. Transaction Obfuscation

If you must use traceable payment systems (like PayPal, Stripe, or your primary bank), create noise.

Methods:

- Make small, harmless purchases that camouflage larger ones.
- Use gift cards (purchased with cash) for online shopping.
- Keep subscription services under a decoy identity to separate them from your financial core.

The goal is not to be completely absent — it's to make your financial patterns unpredictable, fragmented, and unreliable.

7. Income Stealth

How you earn money is just as important as how you spend it. Employment records, payroll systems, and tax filings create obvious trails. But there are ways to add layers of privacy.

Strategies:

- **Freelancing:** Get paid through privacy-respecting platforms (crypto payments, prepaid debit payouts).
- **Side Hustles:** Cash-based gigs (tutoring, repair work, local sales) create income streams outside corporate grids.
- **Royalties & Licensing:** Set up business structures (LLCs, trusts) to separate your identity from earnings.

Pro Tip: If you must use a bank for direct deposits, funnel it into an account you don't use for personal spending. Keep work and life separated.

8. Compartmentalization — Your Financial Firewall

Financial stealth is not about one perfect system. It's about **compartmentalization.** Each part of your financial life should be walled off from the others, so exposure in one doesn't compromise the whole.

- **Account A:** Bills & obligations (minimal funds, automated).
- **Account B:** Daily spending (funded with prepaid cards).
- **Account C:** Private reserves (cash, crypto, physical assets).
- **Account D:** Decoy presence (subscriptions, harmless transactions).

By separating roles, you ensure no single account can be used to map your entire financial behavior.

9. Alternative Stores of Value

Money isn't the only currency worth protecting. Surveillance economies push you to keep everything digital, but stealth thrives on diversification.

Stealth-Friendly Assets:

- Precious metals (gold, silver) — portable, durable, private.
- Tangible goods (tools, food stores, barterable items).
- Privacy-preserving gift cards for big-box stores.

These act as lifeboats if banks freeze accounts or governments impose restrictions.

10. Living Rich, Spending Silent

Financial stealth doesn't mean living in poverty or fear. It means designing a lifestyle where you enjoy freedom without handing your data to surveillance systems.

Imagine:

- Dining out, but paying cash.
- Shopping online, but through prepaid cards or gift codes.
- Earning a living, but through layered structures that protect your identity.

Your digital doppelgänger feeds on every transaction. By cutting off its food supply, you weaken it until it can no longer define who you are.

The Financial Stealth Mindset

- **Every transaction is a choice.** Either it feeds your doppelgänger or starves it.
- **Redundancy is freedom.** Always keep backup forms of payment outside surveillance grids.
- **Patterns expose you.** Vary your methods and keep your systems fluid.

Financial stealth is not about escaping responsibility. It's about reclaiming sovereignty. You pay your bills. You live your life. But you do so on your terms, without leaving yourself exposed to exploitation.

What Comes Next

You now have the blueprints for stealth finance — cash, crypto, prepaid cards, compartmentalization, and alternative assets. But stealth isn't just financial

Chapter 6: Anonymous and Employed — The Myth Destroyed

For decades, the dominant narrative has been: if you want to work, you must be visible. Employers demand résumés, social media checks, and background screenings. Professional networks pressure you to post, like, and share publicly. Entire industries tell you that if you're not "building your personal brand," you'll be left behind.

This is the myth of employment in the surveillance age: **that anonymity and prosperity cannot coexist.**

It is false.

Not only can you remain anonymous while employed — in many cases, anonymity is the very shield that protects your livelihood. Let's dismantle the myth and replace it with a practical blueprint.

The Corporate Mirage of Visibility

Why does the myth exist? Because visibility benefits corporations, not you.

- **Social Media Screening:** Employers trawl LinkedIn, Facebook, and Instagram to judge candidates. They claim it's about "culture fit." In reality, it's about control.
- **Background Checks:** Data brokers make millions selling your history to HR departments.
- **Surveillance-as-Policy:** Increasingly, companies use productivity trackers, keystroke monitors, and even webcam surveillance on remote workers.

The system whispers: *If you have nothing to hide, why resist?* But this flips freedom on its head. Employment should be about skills and value — not about whether your digital doppelgänger pleases the algorithm.

The Truth: Anonymous Work Exists Everywhere

The idea that anonymity kills employment ignores reality. Millions of people already work without handing over their lives:

- **Freelancers and Contractors:** Paid under business names, LLCs, or pseudonyms.
- **Remote Workers:** Using decoy professional profiles while keeping private life sealed away.
- **Creators and Developers:** Earning income under pen names, GitHub handles, or artist identities.
- **Gig Workers:** Driving, delivering, tutoring — transactions that don't require a curated digital persona.

The myth is rooted in corporate tradition, not in necessity.

Step 1: Separate the Masks

The first rule of being anonymous and employed is **compartmentalization.** You maintain two masks:

1. **Professional Mask (Decoy Identity):**
    - A sanitized résumé or LinkedIn profile with only essential career data.
    - A single, clean email address.
    - No personal photos, hobbies, or politics.
2. **Private Mask (True Self):**
    - Your real communications, friendships, and private life.
    - Encrypted, layered, and shielded from employers.

The myth tells you these must overlap. The truth is they should never touch.

Step 2: Use Stealth-Friendly Job Platforms

Not every job marketplace demands exposure. Some thrive on skills over identity.

- **Freelance Hubs:** Upwork, Fiverr, Toptal (sanitized profiles, minimal personal info).
- **Crypto-Paid Marketplaces:** Websites where projects are exchanged for Monero, Bitcoin, or privacy coins.
- **Decentralized Gig Boards:** Forums and communities that value output over résumés.

Pro Tip: Always register with a decoy identity. Never use your main phone or primary email for job platforms.

Step 3: Employment Structures for Stealth

Traditional W-2 employment in the U.S. is heavily exposed — tax forms, payroll systems, benefits. But there are stealth structures you can adopt:

- **LLC or Business Entity:** Instead of working as an individual, invoice as a company. This shields personal details behind a legal veil.
- **Virtual Mailboxes:** Receive official documents at a business address, not your home.
- **Alternative Payment Paths:** Route income through prepaid debit cards or crypto-to-cash exchanges.

These methods let you be employed — even by large companies — without giving them direct access to your private identity.

Step 4: Destroy the "Brand" Myth

The "personal brand" movement tells you that constant visibility equals opportunity. In truth, it equals vulnerability. Every tweet, every post, every photo becomes a liability in the age of cancellation.

You don't need a brand to be employed. You need:

- A verifiable skill set.
- A clear way for employers or clients to reach you.
- A reliable track record (which can be documented under your decoy identity).

Plenty of six-figure contractors, ghostwriters, coders, and consultants have **zero social media presence.** Their brand is their results.

Step 5: Handling Background Checks

One of the most intimidating hurdles is the background check. But even here, anonymity and employment can coexist.

- **Sanitize What You Can:** Use the strategies from Chapter 3 to scrub data brokers.
- **Provide Only Required Data:** Employers often request more than legally necessary. Comply with the minimum, not the maximum.
- **Push Through Entities:** If possible, route contracts through your LLC. Employers then background-check the business, not you.
- **Preempt Surprises:** Run your own background check (via Checkr or GoodHire) to see what employers see. Then clean it up.

Remember: most employers don't need to know who you are in your private life. They just want to know you won't create legal or financial liability for them.

Step 6: Thriving in Stealth Employment

Anonymity isn't just about survival — it's about creating a better working life.

- **No Pressure to Perform Online:** No need to update feeds, post career updates, or curate false images of success.
- **Immunity to Cancel Culture:** Your decoy identity acts as a firewall between your livelihood and personal beliefs.
- **True Freedom of Movement:** You can change jobs, gigs, or careers without dragging a public digital history with you.

In stealth employment, you become untouchable — judged only by the work you deliver, not the shadow you left online.

The Myth Destroyed

The system wants you to believe:

- Anonymity is laziness.
- Employment requires exposure.
- If you're invisible, you'll be irrelevant.

But reality says the opposite:

- Anonymity is power.
- Employment thrives on value, not visibility.
- The less your doppelgänger exists, the freer you are to choose where and how you work.

You can be both **anonymous and employed.** The myth collapses under its own weight once you see the alternatives.

What Comes Next

You now know how to earn, work, and build a career without surrendering your sovereignty. But employment is just one front in the war for freedom

Chapter 7: Social Stealth — Blending In Without Being Consumed

Disappearing from the internet doesn't mean disappearing from life. You are not meant to become a hermit in the woods, hiding from every relationship or opportunity. True stealth is not withdrawal — it's **blending in so well that the system cannot tell what is you and what is smoke.**

This is **social stealth.** The art of moving through the world connected, employed, and engaged while ensuring your digital doppelgänger starves in silence.

The Paradox of Stealth

People assume invisibility equals isolation:

- *If I delete my accounts, how will friends find me?*
- *If I don't post online, will employers think I don't exist?*
- *If I don't share, will my family assume I'm hiding something?*

The paradox is that stealth actually gives you *more freedom* to live socially. You control what is shared, where it is shared, and who sees it. Instead of being consumed by platforms, you curate reality on your own terms.

1. Digital Minimalism — Less Is More

Social stealth begins with digital minimalism: stripping away unnecessary signals so only the essential remains.

Core Practices:

- **One Device Rule:** Keep a primary phone for essentials and a secondary (or burner) for experimental or social interactions.
- **One-to-Many Culling:** If a platform broadcasts to strangers, cut it. Keep only private channels for chosen people.
- **Slow Media:** Replace endless scrolling with deliberate consumption — RSS feeds, newsletters, or direct forums.

Minimalism isn't absence — it's precision. You become visible only where it matters.

2. Friends and Family — Private Without Paranoia

The hardest part of vanishing is handling those closest to you. Family and friends expect to see you online, to tag you, to share pictures. The goal is not to cut them off but to redirect how you're present.

Strategies:

- **Private Groups:** Create small, encrypted group chats (Signal, Session) where updates are shared. This becomes your personal "social media" circle.
- **Photo Control:** If others post pictures of you, politely ask them to remove identifying details (location tags, full names). Frame it as safety, not secrecy.
- **Selective Sharing:** Share stories in person or in private messages. You'll be remembered for authenticity, not filtered feeds.

Pro Tip: Most people overshare because they think it's expected. Once you stop, you'll find they adapt quickly — and may even admire your restraint.

3. Employers and Colleagues — The Decoy Layer

Professional relationships are where stealth and employment intersect. Employers often expect a digital footprint. The key is to provide a **controlled decoy presence.**

- **LinkedIn Decoy:** Keep a bare-bones profile — name, job title, work history, no birthdays, no personal content. Enough to satisfy HR searches, nothing more.
- **Work-Only Email:** A clean, minimal address dedicated solely to professional communications.
- **Compartmentalized Devices:** If your job provides hardware, never mix it with personal use. Assume it is monitored.

This allows you to appear cooperative while keeping your true life sealed away.

4. Public Spaces — The Art of Blending In

Stealth isn't only digital. In physical spaces, surveillance is everywhere: cameras, license plate readers, Wi-Fi trackers. Social stealth means learning to be present without leaving traces.

- **Phones Off in Transit:** Devices constantly ping towers — when possible, leave them behind or switch to airplane mode.
- **Payment Choice:** Pay cash for transportation, meals, and daily errands. A bus ticket bought with coins is invisible; a ride-share app builds a map of your life.
- **Neutral Presence:** In conversations, blend rather than dominate. Share enough to connect, but not enough to archive.

Remember: invisibility isn't silence. It's *normalcy without residue.*

5. Dating, Networking, and Trust

These are areas where people often feel the most exposed. How do you build connections without feeding your doppelgänger?

- **Dating:** Avoid swipe-based apps that harvest data. Instead, use privacy-focused platforms or better yet, in-person introductions. If apps are unavoidable, use decoy profiles with minimal info.
- **Networking:** Focus on small, curated groups (forums, professional associations, encrypted communities). Quality over visibility.
- **Trust Management:** Share pieces of your life selectively, over time. True intimacy doesn't come from data dumps — it comes from shared experiences.

Pro Tip: People respect mystery more than oversharing. Stealth often creates intrigue instead of suspicion.

6. The "Ghosting" Technique

One of the most effective social stealth tactics is **ghosting with grace.** This doesn't mean vanishing from people's lives, but vanishing from **platforms** while staying connected.

- Delete your social accounts gradually, not overnight.
- Provide alternative contact points (phone, encrypted chat).
- Frame it positively: "I'm focusing on real connections," not "I'm hiding from Big Brother."

This ensures you disappear digitally without losing your human network.

7. Living the Blend

The ultimate goal of social stealth is balance:

- You're visible to the people you choose.
- You're invisible to corporations and surveillance systems.
- You move through society like anyone else, but your footprint dissolves as you walk.

When done right, social stealth feels natural. You're not hiding. You're just living without being consumed.

The Social Stealth Mindset

- **Visibility is not connection.** True connection happens offline or in private channels.
- **Normalcy is camouflage.** Appear ordinary; leave no residue.
- **Boundaries are sovereignty.** The less you share by default, the more control you keep.

Social stealth is not about escaping relationships — it's about re-designing them so they belong to *you,* not your doppelgänger.

What Comes Next

Now that you know how to live socially without exposure, it's time to go even deeper.

Because disappearing is power — but turning the system against itself is freedom.

Chapter 8: Shielding from Future Leaks

You've struck the first blows. You've dismantled your digital doppelgänger. You've built stealth systems that let you live, earn, and connect on your terms. But there is a final vulnerability: **time.**

The truth is, data collection never stops. Every day, apps, services, and systems evolve new methods to harvest information. If you do not prepare for the future, the doppelgänger will grow back. Shielding yourself from future leaks is about building a life where **data cannot escape without your permission.**

The Nature of Future Leaks

Leaks aren't always dramatic hacks splashed across headlines. They're often subtle:

- A new app update that quietly changes permissions.
- A subscription service selling user info years after you joined.
- A government mandate that requires companies to share more customer data.
- A family member or colleague who posts about you without your consent.

Future leaks occur not because you've failed, but because the system is designed to erode your defenses. The only solution is to **design resilience.**

1. Build a Leak-Resistant Identity

The best defense is not just scrubbing old accounts — it's creating an identity architecture that limits exposure by design.

Principles:

- **Least Data Necessary:** Give the minimum possible at sign-ups. If they don't need your birthday, don't give it.
- **Alias Layering:** Use decoy details for non-critical accounts (newsletters, forums, shopping).
- **Compartmentalization:** Keep professional, personal, and financial accounts completely siloed.

Pro Tip: Treat your data like currency — only spend it where the return is worth the cost.

2. Harden Your Core Accounts

Some accounts are unavoidable: banking, government, healthcare. These must be shielded like fortresses.

Steps:

- **2FA Everywhere:** Use authenticator apps or hardware keys, not SMS.
- **Password Rotation:** Change them quarterly, using password managers to generate unique strings.
- **Redundancy:** Have backup emails/phones for recovery, but keep them private and compartmentalized.
- **Monitoring:** Set up alerts for logins, password resets, and suspicious activity.

Your core accounts are the crown jewels. Guard them with paranoia.

3. Control the People Around You

Often, leaks don't come from you — they come from others. Friends tagging you in photos, family posting birthdays, coworkers adding details to LinkedIn.

Strategies:

- **Set Boundaries:** Be upfront: "Please don't tag me or post my info online."
- **Educate Quietly:** Explain risks in terms people understand (identity theft, scams).
- **Offer Alternatives:** Share updates through private channels so they don't feel deprived.

This isn't about paranoia — it's about teaching your circle that your privacy is not negotiable.

4. Choose Stealth-Friendly Tech

Your devices are constant leak points. Future-proofing requires adopting hardware and software designed for privacy.

Phones:

- Consider de-Googled Android options (GrapheneOS, CalyxOS).
- Use privacy-focused iOS settings (limit app permissions, disable analytics).

Computers:

- Install Linux or hardened Windows setups.
- Use browsers like Firefox or Brave with tracker-blockers.

Apps:

- Use F-Droid or alternative app stores for open-source software.
- Avoid "free" apps that monetize through surveillance.

Pro Tip: Before installing any app, ask: *Does it need this permission, or is it just extracting data?*

5. Anticipate the Corporate Drift

Services you trust today may betray you tomorrow. Privacy policies change overnight. Companies sell out. Governments force compliance.

Defense Tactics:

- **Regular Policy Audits:** Once a quarter, review the privacy policies of your most-used services.
- **Exit Plans:** Always know how to export, delete, or move data elsewhere.
- **Redundancy:** Keep backups on encrypted drives so you're never hostage to one service.

Assume that anything free will one day turn hostile. Stay ready to move.

6. Automate Your Defenses

Surveillance is constant — your defenses should be, too. Automation reduces human error.

Tools:

- **Data Removal Services:** DeleteMe, Kanary, OneRep — recurring opt-outs from data brokers.
- **Breach Alerts:** Use Have I Been Pwned or paid monitors to alert you when emails appear in leaks.
- **Password Managers:** Auto-generate and store secure credentials.

By automating, you stop leaks before they spread.

7. Future-Proof Your Finances

Financial leaks are inevitable unless you plan ahead. As banks digitize more aggressively, your spending habits will be mined in finer detail.

Steps:

- Continue diversifying into cash, crypto, and tangible assets (see Chapter 5).
- Regularly cycle prepaid cards for online purchases.
- Expect fintech apps to sell data — avoid them unless absolutely necessary.

Pro Tip: Treat every financial service as temporary. Loyalty breeds surveillance.

8. Psychological Shielding

The hardest part of shielding from future leaks isn't technical — it's mental. You must learn to resist convenience culture. Every new app, every new trend, every new platform will tempt you.

Ask yourself before joining:

- What data am I giving away?
- What happens if this leaks five years from now?
- Is the convenience worth permanent exposure?

Most of the time, the answer is no. And saying no becomes your shield.

9. Leak Response Plan

No matter how careful you are, leaks happen. Shielding means being ready for the inevitable.

When a Leak Occurs:

1. Identify what was exposed (email, password, SSN, card).
2. Lock it down immediately (reset, freeze credit, revoke access).
3. Contain the blast radius — check linked accounts.
4. Record the incident in your privacy log.

Think of leaks like fires: small blazes are manageable if caught early.

The Future Belongs to the Shielded

Surveillance thrives on passivity. Leaks grow when no one resists. By shielding yourself today, you don't just erase your past — you block the future from claiming you.

Your goal is not perfection. It is resilience. You won't stop every leak, but you can ensure no leak controls your life.

The Shielding Mindset

- **Default to denial:** If data isn't required, don't give it.
- **Trust is temporary:** Companies change — privacy policies do, too.
- **Prepare for the worst:** Assume every account can be breached. Build redundancies.

Stealth isn't just about the present. It's about building a future where your digital doppelgänger never grows strong enough to enslave you again.

What Comes Next

Now that you've built shields against future leaks, it's time to turn defense into offense.

Chapter 9: Advanced Obfuscation — Confusing, Misleading, and Overwhelming the System

Up until now, you've learned how to delete, conceal, and shield your digital presence. That's the defensive game — crucial, but incomplete. Because while defense protects, it doesn't exhaust the opponent. Surveillance thrives on persistence. To truly reclaim your sovereignty, you must go on offense.

This is the art of **advanced obfuscation**: creating noise, confusion, and disinformation so thick that your digital doppelgänger becomes useless to the very systems that seek to control it.

The Logic of Obfuscation

Surveillance economies run on clarity. The more accurate their data, the more valuable it becomes. If you can't erase everything — and you can't — then your next best strategy is to **pollute it.**

Obfuscation doesn't mean lying recklessly. It means designing deliberate patterns of misdirection so that corporations, algorithms, and data brokers spend more time sorting garbage than exploiting you.

In the age of mass surveillance, invisibility is power. But confusion? That's a weapon.

1. Noise Injection — Burying the Signal

Think of your data like a signal in a sea of noise. The less clear the signal, the less useful it becomes.

Techniques:

- **Fake Search Trails:** Use tools like TrackMeNot (randomized search queries) to flood trackers with noise.
- **Random Click Patterns:** Occasionally click unrelated links or categories to skew algorithmic predictions.
- **Browser Chaff:** Use a second device or VM (virtual machine) solely to generate junk browsing behavior.

Pro Tip: Make the noise plausible. If your history is 99% crypto research and suddenly 1% about penguin breeding, it sticks out. Mix signals subtly so they blend.

2. Synthetic Identities — Ghosts in the Machine

If your real identity feeds the doppelgänger, then why not create shadows to confuse it further?

Synthetic Identity Tactics:

- **Decoy Profiles:** Build harmless accounts with alias names and filler interests (books, gardening, pets).
- **Layered Personas:** Operate multiple low-effort identities that scatter false data across platforms.
- **Email Farms:** Use unique email addresses (via SimpleLogin, AnonAddy, or Proton aliases) for each service. If one leaks, it doesn't compromise the others.

Done well, synthetic identities dilute the surveillance economy, forcing it to waste resources distinguishing between "you" and your ghosts.

3. Metadata Manipulation — Poisoning the Records

Content isn't the only thing that matters — **metadata is the skeleton of surveillance.** By manipulating metadata, you poison the skeleton itself.

Methods:

- **Photo Obfuscation:** Strip EXIF data before posting; add fake metadata if you want to mislead.
- **VPN Rotation:** Change locations frequently to suggest movement across borders.
- **Device Spoofing:** Tools exist to fake operating system, browser type, or hardware signatures.

Imagine a doppelgänger whose logs show you in Paris, Tokyo, and São Paulo within the same 24 hours. To an algorithm, you become unreliable.

4. Algorithm Sabotage — Feeding the Beast Junk Food

Recommendation engines are surveillance in disguise. YouTube, Netflix, Amazon — all designed to profile your desires. Sabotage them by feeding garbage data.

- Watch random genres with throwaway accounts.
- Leave conflicting reviews (five stars for one thing, one star for the opposite).
- Follow contradictory interests (fitness equipment + junk food).

The result? An algorithm so confused it cannot sell, predict, or manipulate you effectively.

5. Decentralized Disruption

Beyond personal tactics, obfuscation can be collective. Communities of privacy-minded users already use **data pollution** to overwhelm surveillance systems.

- **Crowdsourced Obfuscation Tools:** Plugins that auto-generate random queries for everyone.
- **Anonymity Networks:** Tor, I2P, Freenet — collective bandwidth makes every user harder to isolate.
- **Open Source Sabotage:** Scripts and bots that spam data brokers with inaccurate records.

When thousands inject noise at once, surveillance collapses under its own weight.

6. Camouflage in Normalcy

Paradoxically, the best obfuscation is often blending in. If you look too extreme, you stand out. If you mimic normal users but feed subtle contradictions, you vanish inside the herd.

Strategies:

- Maintain one sanitized professional account.
- Share mundane interests on a decoy identity (food pics, travel quotes).
- Obfuscate only in ways that mimic human unpredictability.

Obfuscation is camouflage. Done correctly, you don't vanish into black — you vanish into the crowd.

7. Data Sabotage as Long-Term Strategy

Over time, the effect of advanced obfuscation compounds. Algorithms trained on poisoned data drift into nonsense. Profiles sold by brokers degrade in accuracy. Your doppelgänger becomes a broken mirror — a reflection no one can trust.

This doesn't just protect you. It protects everyone downstream. When enough people sabotage the system, the data economy itself begins to fail.

8. Ethical Edge

Some may wonder: *Isn't this dishonest?* The answer depends on perspective. Corporations built the surveillance economy on manipulation without consent. Obfuscation is not lying — it is **counter-surveillance.** It is reclaiming balance in a system stacked against the individual.

Think of it not as deception but as **defense by distortion.**

The Obfuscation Mindset

- **Confusion is currency.** The less predictable you are, the less exploitable you become.
- **Noise is shield.** Flood the system until your true self disappears.
- **Camouflage is survival.** Blend in, but bend reality beneath the surface.

Obfuscation completes the cycle: from erasure (past), to shielding (present), to sabotage (future).

What Comes Next

You've learned how to confuse and overwhelm surveillance systems. But stealth is not just about surviving algorithms — it's about living fully and freely.

Chapter 10: Living Freely, Seen by No One

You began this journey by realizing a truth few dare to face: you've been watched. Every click, purchase, and conversation was feeding a ghostly version of yourself — a doppelgänger that existed not to serve you, but to serve the system.

You dismantled it. You starved it. You poisoned it with obfuscation until it became unreliable, a broken mirror that no longer controlled your reflection. You shielded yourself from future leaks and armed yourself with tools to stay invisible.

But the ultimate goal was never disappearance for its own sake. It was **freedom.**

To live freely, seen by no one, is to design a life where you exist fully — not diminished, not erased — but beyond the reach of those who would capture and commodify you.

1. Redefining Freedom in the Surveillance Age

For most people, freedom is a slogan. They believe they are free because they can speak, spend, or travel — without realizing every act is tagged, tracked, and scored.

True freedom begins when you sever the link between **who you are** and **what they know.**

You are free when:

- Your choices are not shaped by ads that know your fears.
- Your relationships aren't judged by old posts or hidden records.
- Your income, identity, and daily life don't depend on platforms you cannot control.

You are free when you are invisible to those who would use your shadow to cage you.

2. The Joy of Selective Visibility

Living unseen doesn't mean hiding in darkness. It means **choosing where you shine.**

- You can share moments with trusted friends — privately, securely, without platforms mining them.
- You can appear professional when you want — through controlled decoys that reveal only what's necessary.
- You can create, love, and grow without being reduced to "content."

Selective visibility is the art of being a lighthouse, not a billboard. You decide when and where to be seen — and when to vanish.

3. Wealth Without Chains

Financial stealth (Chapter 5) wasn't about survival. It was about building wealth that doesn't enslave you.

Living freely means:

- Using cash without apology.
- Holding assets that can't be frozen with a keystroke.
- Earning income through structures that protect your name, not exploit it.

Wealth is not just numbers on a screen. True wealth is resilience: the ability to move, adapt, and thrive even when the system tries to close in.

4. Relationships Without Residue

One of the greatest myths is that connection requires constant posting. In reality, the strongest relationships thrive in privacy.

- Families bond deeper in face-to-face time than in tagged photos.
- Friendships grow stronger when they're not performed for an audience.
- Love flourishes in mystery — in what's shared intimately, not publicly.

Living freely means your relationships exist in the real world, not as curated fragments owned by corporations.

5. Work Without Surveillance

You've destroyed the myth that anonymity kills employment (Chapter 6). In truth, stealth makes you a stronger worker: focused, unburdened, untouchable by digital witch hunts.

- Your career becomes defined by results, not rumors.
- Your value is measured in skill, not in "likes" or follows.
- Your livelihood exists behind firewalls of protection, out of reach of weaponized data.

Employment becomes what it always should have been: an exchange of value, not a surrender of privacy.

6. The Lifestyle of a Ghost in Plain Sight

Living unseen is not isolation — it is integration without exposure. A ghost in plain sight moves freely, unnoticed, because nothing clings to them.

Practical daily habits for living as a ghost:

- Pay cash in person; use decoys online.
- Speak openly in encrypted channels; leave nothing on public feeds.
- Walk through society with ordinary normalcy, but leave no residue.

You are there, fully alive, but when the system looks for you, it finds only fog.

7. The Psychological Shift

Perhaps the greatest transformation isn't technical — it's internal.

To live freely, seen by no one, is to no longer crave the validation of the feed, the scoreboard, the digital applause. It is to reclaim the silence of sovereignty.

At first, the quiet feels strange. No notifications, no algorithm pushing the next dopamine hit. But then something changes:

- Your attention returns to what matters.
- Your creativity deepens without the pressure of performance.
- Your identity becomes yours alone — unshaped by invisible observers.

Freedom is not the absence of attention. It is the presence of control.

8. The Future of the Invisible

The world will only grow more intrusive. AI surveillance, predictive policing, biometric tracking — the doppelgänger will evolve new tricks. But those who master stealth will always stay one step ahead.

The invisible become ungovernable. Not in chaos, but in sovereignty. They live lives corporations cannot predict, governments cannot score, and algorithms cannot sell.

Invisibility is not the end of freedom. It is the beginning of a new kind of human power.

The Vanisher's Code

To live freely, seen by no one, you must remember three unbreakable truths:

1. **Control your data, or it will control you.**
2. **Share selectively, and you will never be enslaved by exposure.**
3. **Confuse the system, and you will always be freer than the visible.**

This is the code of the Vanisher. Not running away. Not living in fear. But reclaiming the ancient right to live as you choose, beyond the chains of watchers and algorithms.

Closing Words

You are not your doppelgänger. You are not your feeds. You are not your leaks or your histories.

You are more.

You are a sovereign human being in a digital age that has forgotten what sovereignty means. And now you hold the blueprint to reclaim it.

Disappear from the systems that never deserved you.
Reappear only where you choose.
Live fully.
Live freely.
Live seen by no one.

Appendix A: Platforms and Tools for Digital Disappearance

This appendix is designed to be your quick-access field guide. While chapters in this book explore the philosophy and practice of vanishing in detail, here you'll find a curated directory of **platforms, tools, and services** that can help you dismantle your digital doppelgänger, shield your identity, and live unseen.

Note: Technology changes rapidly. Always verify privacy policies and ensure that tools haven't been compromised or acquired by surveillance-oriented corporations before use.

1. Secure Communication

Encrypted Messaging

- **Signal** — Gold standard for end-to-end encryption, minimal metadata, supports disappearing messages.
- **Session** — Decentralized, anonymous messaging app that doesn't require a phone number.
- **Threema** — Paid, privacy-first messenger, stores minimal user data.

Encrypted Email

- **ProtonMail** — Swiss-based, zero-access encryption, integrates with ProtonVPN.
- **Tutanota** — Germany-based, end-to-end encrypted, includes encrypted calendars and contacts.
- **Mailbox.org** — Business-friendly encrypted email with productivity tools.

Pro Tip: Always create separate email identities for different roles (professional, financial, social, decoy).

2. Browsers and Search Engines

Privacy Browsers

- **Firefox** (with extensions: uBlock Origin, Privacy Badger, NoScript, Multi-Account Containers).
- **Brave** — Built-in tracker blocking, Tor integration for private tabs.
- **Tor Browser** — Highest anonymity, routes traffic through multiple relays, ideal for sensitive research.

Search Engines

- **DuckDuckGo** — No tracking, neutral search results.
- **Startpage** — Pulls Google results without tracking or storing your queries.
- **SearXNG** — Open-source meta-search engine, can be self-hosted.

Pro Tip: Rotate browsers for different activities. Never mix professional, personal, and stealth use in the same browser.

3. VPNs and Network Privacy

VPN Services

- **Mullvad** — Anonymous accounts (no email required), cash or crypto payments.
- **ProtonVPN** — High-security infrastructure, integrates with Proton ecosystem.
- **IVPN** — Transparent ownership, multi-hop routing for layered anonymity.

Other Network Tools

- **Tor Network** — For maximum anonymity, though slower.
- **I2P** — An alternative anonymity network for peer-to-peer communication.
- **Psiphon** — Circumvents censorship in restrictive regions.

Pro Tip: Always choose VPN providers audited for "no logs" policies. Free VPNs often sell your data.

4. Identity and Obfuscation Tools

Alias Management

- **SimpleLogin** — Email alias manager, creates unlimited "burner" emails.
- **AnonAddy** — Privacy-focused email forwarding with aliases.
- **MySudo** — Multiple phone numbers and email identities in one app.

Fake Identity Generators

- **Fakenamegenerator.com** — Generates synthetic identities for testing or decoys.
- **Privacy.com** — Creates virtual, disposable debit cards tied to aliases.
- **Hushed** — Burner phone numbers for temporary use.

Pro Tip: Keep an encrypted spreadsheet of your aliases to avoid cross-contamination.

5. Data Erasure and Leak Management

Data Broker Removal

- **DeleteMe (Abine)** — Subscription service for recurring removal from people search sites.
- **Kanary** — Automates opt-outs from data brokers, regularly re-checks.
- **OneRep** — Focused on U.S. broker removals, simple interface.

Breach Monitoring

- **Have I Been Pwned** — Free tool to check if your email/phone appears in leaks.
- **Firefox Monitor** — Alerts when your accounts are caught in breaches.
- **SpyCloud** — Paid service for professional leak monitoring.

Pro Tip: Schedule reminders to re-run data broker removals every 6–12 months.

6. Financial Stealth Tools

Cash Alternatives

- **Prepaid Debit Cards** (store-bought with cash) — For anonymous online shopping.
- **Gift Cards** — Large retailers like Amazon or Visa/Mastercard gift cards can be purchased with cash.

Cryptocurrency

- **Monero (XMR)** — Privacy coin with untraceable transactions.
- **Zcash (ZEC)** — Shielded transaction option for strong anonymity.
- **Wasabi Wallet (for Bitcoin)** — CoinJoin transactions to obscure BTC history.

Pro Tip: Never buy crypto directly on ID-verified exchanges if anonymity is your goal. Use peer-to-peer or cash-to-crypto services instead.

7. Device and Operating Systems

Secure Operating Systems

- **Qubes OS** — Security-focused, isolates apps in separate virtual machines.
- **Tails OS** — Live boot OS that routes all traffic through Tor; leaves no trace on device.
- **Linux (Debian, Ubuntu, Fedora)** — Open-source alternatives to Windows/MacOS, more customizable for privacy.

Mobile OS Options

- **GrapheneOS** — Hardened Android, ideal for privacy-first users.
- **CalyxOS** — Privacy-enhanced Android with easier usability.
- **LineageOS** — Open-source Android variant with fewer trackers.

Pro Tip: Use "de-Googled" phones for stealth; keep mainstream devices strictly compartmentalized.

8. Metadata and File Obfuscation

Metadata Removal

- **ExifTool** — Removes geotags and metadata from photos and files.
- **MAT2 (Metadata Anonymisation Toolkit)** — Open-source tool for stripping metadata.

File Encryption

- **VeraCrypt** — Create encrypted containers for sensitive files.
- **Cryptomator** — Encrypts files synced to cloud storage.
- **KeePassXC** — Open-source password manager with local encrypted vaults.

Pro Tip: Strip metadata before sharing any media — even private photos can reveal location, time, and device info.

9. Automation for Privacy Maintenance

- **RoboForm / Bitwarden** — Secure password managers for automating strong password use.
- **Cron Jobs + Scripts** — For tech-savvy users: automated cache clearing, data wiping.
- **Recurring Calendar Reminders** — Schedule "privacy sweeps" every 3–6 months.

Pro Tip: Treat privacy like hygiene — regular small cleanups prevent catastrophic leaks later.

10. The Human Layer

No platform can fully protect you without discipline. Your habits are the final shield.

- Always ask: *Do they need this information, or am I giving it away for free?*
- Default to "deny" on permissions.
- Use compartmentalization: never mix personal, professional, and stealth lives.

Technology is only as strong as the mindset behind it.

Final Note

This appendix is not a static list — it is a **living arsenal.** The platforms that protect you today may betray you tomorrow through acquisition, policy change, or compromise. The key is vigilance.

Stay updated. Rotate tools. Keep your shields sharp.

Because the system evolves, but so can you.

Appendix B: Identity Safety Plan

Anonymity is not a one-time action — it is a lifestyle. Your identity safety requires a living framework, something you can rely on whether you're calmly managing accounts or urgently responding to a breach. This appendix is your **Identity Safety Plan**: a structured guide to keeping your sovereignty intact no matter what threats arise.

1. The Core Principles of Identity Safety

Before diving into steps, keep these three rules as your compass:

1. **Minimize Exposure:** Give the least possible personal data to any service.
2. **Compartmentalize:** Keep professional, financial, social, and stealth identities separate.
3. **Monitor and Respond:** Regularly check for leaks and act immediately when something slips.

2. Daily Identity Habits

These are your non-negotiable daily practices. Over time, they become second nature:

- **Use Encrypted Channels:** Signal for messaging, Proton/Tutanota for email.
- **Check Permissions:** Deny location/microphone access unless strictly required.
- **Browse Safely:** Use a privacy browser (Brave, Firefox with extensions, or Tor) and connect through VPN.
- **Password Hygiene:** Always use a password manager with unique, complex credentials for every login.
- **Minimal Social Sharing:** Never post birthdays, addresses, or financial details — even indirectly.

Pro Tip: Treat every login as a potential leak — ask, *"What am I revealing here?"*

3. Weekly Maintenance

Every week, run through a short identity audit:

- **Clear Histories:** Delete browsing histories, app caches, and unused cookies.
- **Check for Leaks:** Run your email/phone through *Have I Been Pwned.*
- **Alias Rotation:** Use new burner emails/phone numbers for fresh accounts.
- **Update Decoys:** Post benign content to your decoy identity to maintain camouflage.

Think of weekly maintenance as brushing your teeth: small actions that prevent long-term damage.

4. Monthly Safeguards

At the end of each month, do a deeper sweep:

- **Password Rotation:** Change credentials for your core accounts (bank, healthcare, government).
- **Audit Financial Statements:** Look for suspicious micro-transactions or unusual charges.
- **Review Subscriptions:** Cancel or reassign services that don't need your real information.
- **Data Broker Sweep:** Re-check Whitepages, Spokeo, Intelius, etc., and file removal requests.

Pro Tip: Create an encrypted calendar (Proton Calendar, Tutanota) with reminders for each monthly task.

5. Quarterly Identity Drill

Every three months, test your defenses as if you were the attacker.

- **Run a Background Check:** Use sites like BeenVerified or Intelius to see what strangers find about you.
- **Search Yourself Deeply:** Google/Bing your name, reverse-image search old photos, check cached results.
- **Breach Simulation:** Test whether your alias accounts are cross-linked by intentionally searching for their overlap.
- **Device Checkup:** Update operating systems, clear old Wi-Fi networks, rotate advertising IDs.

The quarterly drill shows you exactly how exposed you look to outsiders.

6. Annual Reset

Once a year, commit to a full reset of your privacy systems:

- **New Hardware or OS:** If possible, rotate into a fresh device or reflash your system.
- **Crypto & Finance Rotation:** Move assets into fresh wallets/accounts, purge old prepaid cards.
- **Alias Rebuild:** Retire old decoys and seed new ones with fresh histories.
- **Hard Data Review:** Request credit reports, government records, and purge outdated personal files.

Think of this as a spring cleaning for your digital existence.

7. Crisis Response Plan

Leaks are inevitable. What matters is **how you respond.** Use this sequence when your data is exposed:

Step 1: Contain

- Change all compromised passwords immediately.
- Freeze accounts/cards if financial data is involved.
- Notify your bank and monitor for fraudulent activity.

Step 2: Erase

- Use removal tools (DeleteMe, Kanary, OneRep) to scrub newly exposed data.
- Contact platforms directly to request removal of posted or leaked details.

Step 3: Fortify

- Rotate into new aliases, numbers, or devices.
- Enable stronger protections (hardware keys, additional encryption).

Step 4: Log

- Record the incident in your privacy journal/spreadsheet: what was leaked, when, and what actions you took.
- Use this record to prevent repeat vulnerabilities.

8. The Privacy Toolkit Essentials

Keep a dedicated "Identity Safety Toolkit" on hand — either on an encrypted USB drive or offline notebook. It should include:

- Master list of your aliases (encrypted).
- List of removal request links for major data brokers.
- Encrypted backup of critical IDs, financials, and recovery codes.
- Offline copies of privacy guides and your own action plan.

This ensures you're ready to respond even if systems are offline or compromised.

9. The Mindset Shift

Technology protects you only as much as your mindset does. Living with identity safety is not paranoia — it is sovereignty.

- **Always Assume Risk:** No account is perfectly secure.
- **Treat Convenience with Suspicion:** If it's "free and easy," it's extracting something.
- **Stay Disciplined:** Habits, not tools, are the strongest shield.

Final Reminder

Your digital doppelgänger cannot be erased once and for all — but it can be starved, weakened, and broken. This Identity Safety Plan is your shield. By following daily, weekly, monthly, and crisis protocols, you ensure your true self remains untouched while only shadows move through the system.

To live freely, seen by no one, you must not only disappear once — you must disappear **every day.**

Appendix C: A 90-Day Disappearance Plan

This 90-day plan is your **action map** — a structured journey from exposed to invisible. It breaks the overwhelming project of digital disappearance into weekly goals so you can dismantle your digital doppelgänger, shield your identity, and begin living freely, seen by no one.

Phase 1: Erasure (Days 1–30)

Objective: Cut off the fuel supply to your digital doppelgänger by scrubbing old data and closing forgotten accounts.

Week 1: The Audit

- Create an encrypted spreadsheet (KeePassXC, VeraCrypt) to track accounts, aliases, and removals.
- List all email addresses you've ever used.
- Run your emails/phone numbers through **Have I Been Pwned** to identify breaches.
- Google and Bing yourself — note every page, image, and cached record.

Week 2: Forgotten Accounts

- Recover or delete abandoned emails (Yahoo, AOL, Hotmail, etc.).
- Shut down or sanitize old social media profiles (MySpace, Tumblr, LiveJournal).
- Search for your name on **Spokeo, Whitepages, Intelius, BeenVerified** — log all appearances.

Week 3: Broker Purge

- Begin opt-outs from data brokers using guides or services like **DeleteMe** or **Kanary.**
- Remove yourself from Google Maps contributions (reviews, old locations).
- File removal requests with Google's "Outdated Content" tool for search results.

Week 4: Cloud & App Sweep

- Audit all cloud accounts: Dropbox, Google Drive, iCloud. Delete or encrypt sensitive files.
- Check your devices for unused apps — uninstall anything you don't need.
- Revoke unnecessary app permissions (location, microphone, camera).

Phase 2: Shielding (Days 31–60)

Objective: Harden your present identity and set up defensive systems to prevent new leaks.

Week 5: Fortress Accounts

- Change passwords on all core accounts (banking, healthcare, government).
- Enable **2FA** with authenticator apps or hardware keys.
- Create a clean, minimal **professional email** for employment/official use.

Week 6: Device Hardening

- Switch your main browser to **Firefox with uBlock Origin, Privacy Badger, and NoScript.**
- Install a **VPN** (Mullvad, ProtonVPN, IVPN) on all devices.
- Rotate advertising IDs on your phone; disable analytics and background tracking.

Week 7: Communication Shift

- Migrate to **Signal** or **Session** for private messaging.
- Set disappearing messages as default.
- Move sensitive conversations to encrypted email (ProtonMail, Tutanota).

Week 8: Social Shielding

- Inform close family/friends not to post or tag you without permission.
- Create a sanitized **LinkedIn decoy** (basic career info only).
- Retire or lock down personal accounts, leaving only private circles.

Phase 3: Obfuscation (Days 61–90)

Objective: Confuse and overwhelm the system so any data that leaks is polluted and useless.

Week 9: Alias & Decoys

- Generate new alias emails using **SimpleLogin** or **AnonAddy.**
- Seed one or two harmless decoy identities (hobbies, interests, professional mask).
- Set up prepaid cards or gift cards for future online purchases.

Week 10: Metadata & Noise

- Install **ExifTool** or MAT2 to strip metadata from all media before sharing.
- Begin using **TrackMeNot** or random query tools to inject noise into search profiles.
- Occasionally run browsing sessions in Tor or a virtual machine to diversify signals.

Week 11: Financial Stealth

- Transition some payments to prepaid debit cards.
- Experiment with Monero or Zcash for private crypto transactions.
- Compartmentalize: separate accounts for bills, daily spending, reserves, and decoy use.

Week 12: Obfuscation Drill

- Run a self-check: Google yourself, run background checks, search people-finder sites.
- Note what's still visible and whether your doppelgänger looks fractured.
- Add noise where traces remain — update decoys, flood irrelevant signals, rotate aliases.

After 90 Days: The New Normal

By the end of this plan, you will have:

- Erased your most dangerous digital shadows.
- Hardened your core accounts and devices.
- Built alias systems and decoys for camouflage.
- Seeded noise and obfuscation into surveillance pipelines.

But disappearance is not an end point — it's a practice. Treat this plan as a foundation. From here, maintain your identity safety with:

- **Weekly hygiene** (cache clearing, leak checks).
- **Quarterly drills** (background searches, device audits).
- **Annual resets** (hardware, aliases, and financial rotation).

Final Word

The system wants you predictable, exposed, and owned. In 90 days, you can become the opposite: resilient, invisible, ungovernable.

The journey doesn't end here. It deepens. Each choice you make — each login denied, each piece of data withheld, each layer of camouflage — is another step into freedom.

Disappear once.

Maintain forever.

Live freely, seen by no one.

Message from the Author:

I hope you enjoyed this book, I love astrology and knew there was not a book such as this out on the shelf. I love metaphysical items as well. Please check out my other books:

-Life of Government Benefits

-My life of Hell

-My life with Hydrocephalus

-Red Sky

-World Domination:Woman's rule

-World Domination:Woman's Rule 2: The War

-Life and Banishment of Apophis: book 1

-The Kidney Friendly Diet

-The Ultimate Hemp Cookbook

-Creating a Dispensary(legally)

-Cleanliness throughout life: the importance of showering from childhood to adulthood.

-Strong Roots: The Risks of Overcoddling children

-Hemp Horoscopes: Cosmic Insights and Earthly Healing

- Celestial Hemp Navigating the Zodiac: Through the Green Cosmos

-Astrological Hemp: Aligning The Stars with Earth's Ancient Herb

-The Astrological Guide to Hemp: Stars, Signs, and Sacred Leaves

-Green Growth: Innovative Marketing Strategies for your Hemp Products and Dispensary

-Cosmic Cannabis

-Astrological Munchies

-Henry The Hemp

-Zodiacal Roots: The Astrological Soul Of Hemp

- Green Constellations: Intersection of Hemp and Zodiac

-Hemp in The Houses: An astrological Adventure Through The Cannabis Galaxy

-Galactic Ganja Guide

Heavenly Hemp

Zodiac Leaves
Doctor Who Astrology
Cannastrology
Stellar Satvias and Cosmic Indicas
Celestial Cannabis: A Zodiac Journey
AstroHerbology: The Sky and The Soil: Volume 1
AstroHerbology:Celestial Cannabis:Volume 2
Cosmic Cannabis Cultivation
The Starry Guide to Herbal Harmony: Volume 1
The Starry Guide to Herbal Harmony: Cannabis Universe: Volume 2
Yugioh Astrology: Astrological Guide to Deck, Duels and more
Nightmare Mansion: Echoes of The Abyss
Nightmare Mansion 2: Legacy of Shadows
Nightmare Mansion 3: Shadows of the Forgotten
Nightmare Mansion 4: Echoes of the Damned
The Life and Banishment of Apophis: Book 2
Nightmare Mansion: Halls of Despair
Healing with Herb: Cannabis and Hydrocephalus
Planetary Pot: Aligning with Astrological Herbs: Volume 1
Fast Track to Freedom: 30 Days to Financial Independence Using AI, Assets, and Agile Hustles
Cosmic Hemp Pathways
How to Become Financially Free in 30 Days: 10,000 Paths to Prosperity
Zodiacal Herbage: Astrological Insights: Volume 1
Nightmare Mansion: Whispers in the Walls
The Daleks Invade Atlantis
Henry the hemp and Hydrocephalus

10X The Kidney Friendly Diet
Cannabis Universe: Adult coloring book
Hemp Astrology: The Healing Power of the Stars

Zodiacal Herbage: Astrological Insights: Cannabis Universe: Volume 2

Planetary Pot: Aligning with Astrological Herbs: Cannabis Universes: Volume 2

Doctor Who: Convergence Protocol – The Replicator War

Nightmare Mansion: Curse of the Blood Moon

The Celestial Stoner: A Guide to the Zodiac

Cosmic Pleasures: Sex Toy Astrology for Every Sign

Hydrocephalus Astrology: Navigating the Stars and Healing Waters

Lapis and the Mischievous Chocolate Bar

Celestial Positions: Sexual Astrology for Every Sign

Apophis's Shadow Work Journal: **:** A Journey of Self-Discovery and Healing

Kinky Cosmos: Sexual Kink Astrology for Every Sign

Digital Cosmos: The Astrological Digimon Compendium

Stellar Seeds: The Cosmic Guide to Growing with Astrology

Apophis's Daily Gratitude Journal

Cat Astrology: Feline Mysteries of the Cosmos

The Cosmic Kama Sutra: An Astrological Guide to Sexual Positions

Unleash Your Potential: A Guided Journal Powered by AI Insights

Whispers of the Enchanted Grove

Cosmic Pleasures: An Astrological Guide to Sexual Kinks

369, 12 Manifestation Journal

Whisper of the nocturne journal(blank journal for writing or drawing)

The Boogey Book

Locked In Reflection: A Chastity Journey Through Locktober

Generating Wealth Quickly:How to Generate $100,000 in 24 Hours

Star Magic: Harness the Power of the Universe

The Flatulence Chronicles: A Fart Journal for Self-Discovery

The Doctor and The Death Moth

Seize the Day: A Personal Seizure Tracking Journal

The Ultimate Boogeyman Safari: A Journey into the Boogie World and Beyond

Whispers of Samhain: 1,000 Spells of Love, Luck, and Lunar Magic: Samhain Spell Book

Apophis's guides:Witch's Spellbook Crafting Guide for Halloween

Frost & Flame: The Enchanted Yule Grimoire of 1000 Winter Spells

The Ultimate Boogey Goo Guide & Spooky Activities for Halloween Fun

Harmony of the Scales: A Libra's Spellcraft for Balance and Beauty

The Enchanted Advent: 36 Days of Christmas Wonders

Nightmare Mansion: The Labyrinth of Screams

Harvest of Enchantment: 1,000 Spells of Gratitude, Love, and Fortune for Thanksgiving

The Boogey Chronicles: A Journal of Nightly Encounters and Shadowy Secrets

The 12 Days of Financial Freedom: A Step-by-Step Christmas Countdown to Transform Your Finances

Sigil of the Eternal Spiral Blank Journal

A Christmas Feast: Timeless Recipes for Every Meal

Holiday Stress-Free Solutions: A Survival Guide to Thriving During the Festive Season

Yu-Gi-Oh! Holiday Gifting Mastery: The Ultimate Guide for Fans and Newcomers Alike

Holiday Harmony: A Hydrocephalus Survival Guide for the Festive Season

Celestial Craft: The Witch's Almanac for 2025 – A Cosmic Guide to Manifestations, Moons, and Mystical Events

Doctor Who: The Toymaker's Winter Wonderland

Tulsa King Unveiled: A Thrilling Guide to Stallone's Mafia Masterpiece

Pendulum Craft: A Complete Guide to Crafting and Using Personalized Divination Tools

Nightmare Mansion: Santa's Eternal Eve

Starlight Noel: A Cosmic Journey through Christmas Mysteries

The Dark Architect: Unlocking the Blueprint of Existence

Surviving the Embrace: The Ultimate Guide to Encounters with The Hugging Molly

The Enchanted Codex: Secrets of the Craft for Witches, Wiccans, and Pagans

Harvest of Gratitude: A Complete Thanksgiving Guide

Yuletide Essentials: A Complete Guide to an Authentic and Magical Christmas

Celestial Smokes: A Cosmic Guide to Cigars and Astrology

Living in Balance: A Comprehensive Survival Guide to Thriving with Diabetes Insipidus

Cosmic Symbiosis: The Venom Zodiac Chronicles

The Cursed Paw of Ambition

Cosmic Symbiosis: The Astrological Venom Journal

Celestial Wonders Unfold: A Stargazer's Guide to the Cosmos (2024-2029)

The Ultimate Black Friday Prepper's Guide: Mastering Shopping Strategies and Savings

Cosmic Sales: The Astrological Guide to Black Friday Shopping

Legends of the Corn Mother and Other Harvest Myths

Whispers of the Harvest: The Corn Mother's Journal

The Evergreen Spellbook

The Doctor Meets the Boogeyman

The White Witch of Rose Hall's SpellBook

The Gingerbread Golem's Shadow: A Study in Sweet Darkness

The Gingerbread Golem Codex: An Academic Exploration of Sweet Myths

The Gingerbread Golem Grimoire: Sweet Magicks and Spells for the Festive Witch

The Curse of the Gingerbread Golem

10-minute Christmas Crafts for kids

Christmas Crisis Solutions: The Ultimate Last-Minute Survival Guide

Gingerbread Golem Recipes: Holiday Treats with a Magical Twist

The Infinite Key: Unlocking Mystical Secrets of the Ages

Enchanted Yule: A Wiccan and Pagan Guide to a Magical and Memorable Season

Dinosaurs of Power: Unlocking Ancient Magick

Astro-Dinos: The Cosmic Guide to Prehistoric Wisdom

Gallifrey's Yule Logs: A Festive Doctor Who Cookbook

The Dino Grimoire: Secrets of Prehistoric Magick

The Gift They Never Knew They Needed

The Gingerbread Golem's Culinary Alchemy: Enchanting Recipes for a Sweetly Dark Feast

A Time Lord Christmas: Holiday Adventures with the Doctor

Krampusproofing Your Home: Defensive Strategies for Yule

Silent Frights: A Collection of Christmas Creepypastas to Chill Your Bones

Santa Raptor's Jolly Carnage: A Dino-Claus Christmas Tale

Prehistoric Palettes: A Dino Wicca Coloring Journey

The Christmas Wishkeeper Chronicles

The Starlight Sleigh: A Holiday Journey

Elf Secrets: The True Magic of the North Pole

Candy Cane Conjurations

Cooking with Kids: Recipes Under 20 Minutes

Doctor Who: The TARDIS Confiscation

The Anxiety First Aid Kit: Quick Tools to Calm Your Mind

Frosty Whispers: A Winter's Tale

The Infinite Key: Unlocking the Secrets to Prosperity, Resilience, and Purpose

The Grasping Void: Why You'll Regret This Purchase

Astrology for Busy Bees: Star Signs Simplified

The Instant Focus Formula: Cut Through the Noise

The Secret Language of Colors: Unlocking the Emotional Codes

Sacred Fossil Chronicles: Blank Journal

The Christmas Cottage Miracle

Feeding Frenzy: Graboid-Inspired Recipes

Manifest in Minutes: The Quick Law of Attraction Guide

The Symbiote Chronicles: Doctor Who's Venomous Journey

Think Tiny, Grow Big: The Minimalist Mindset

The Energy Key: Unlocking Limitless Motivation

New Year, New Magic: Manifesting Your Best Year Yet

Unstoppable You: Mastering Confidence in Minutes

Infinite Energy: The Secret to Never Feeling Drained

Lightning Focus: Mastering the Art of Productivity in a Distracted World

Saturnalia Manifestation Magick: A Guide to Unlocking Abundance During the Solstice

Graboids and Garland: The Ultimate Tremors-Themed Christmas Guide

12 Nights of Holiday Magic

The Power of Pause: 60-Second Mindfulness Practices

The Quick Reset: How to Reclaim Your Life After Burnout

The Shadow Eater: A Tale of Despair and Survival

The Micro-Mastery Method: Transform Your Skills in Just Minutes a Day

Reclaiming Time: How to Live More by Doing Less

Chronovore: The Eternal Nexus

The Mind Reset: Unlocking Your Inner Peace in a Chaotic World

Confidence Code: Building Unshakable Self-Belief

Baby the Vampire Terrier
Baby the Vampire Terrier's Christmas Adventure
Celestial Streams: The Content Creator's Astrology Manual
The Wealth Whisperer: Unlocking Abundance with Everyday Actions
The Energy Equation: Maximize Your Output Without Burning Out
The Happiness Algorithm: Science-Backed Steps to Joyful Living
Stress-Free Success: Achieving Goals Without Anxiety
Mindful Wealth: The New Blueprint for Financial Freedom
The Festive Flavors of New Year: A Culinary Celebration
The Master's Gambit: Keys of Eternal Power
Shadowed Secrets: Groundhog Day Mysteries
Beneath the Burrow: Lessons from the Groundhog
Spring's Whispers: The Groundhog's Prediction
The Limitless Mindset: Unlock Your Untapped Potential
The Focus Funnel: How to Cut Through Chaos and Get Results
Bold Moves: Building Courage to Live on Your Terms
The Daily Shift: Simple Practices for Lasting Transformation
The Quarter-Life Reset: Thriving in Your 20s and 30s
The Art of Shadowplay: Building Your Own Personal Myth
The Eternal Loop: Finding Purpose in Repetition
Burrowing Wisdom: Life Lessons from the Groundhog
Shadow Work: A Groundhog Day Perspective
Love in Bloom: 5-Minute Romantic Gestures
The Shadowspell Codex: Secrets of Forbidden Magick
The Burnout Cure: Finding Balance in a Busy World
The Groundhog Prophecy: Unlocking Seasonal Secrets
Nog Tales: The Spirited History of Eggnog
Six More Weeks: Embracing Seasonal Transitions
The Lumivian Chronicles: Fragments of the Fifth Dimension
Money on Your Mind: A Beginner's Guide to Wealth
The Focus Fix: Breaking Through Distraction

January's Spirit Keepers: Mystical Protectors of the Cold
Creativity Unchained: Unlocking Your Wildest Ideas in 2025
Manifestation Mastery: 365 Days to Rewrite Your Reality
The Groundhog's Mirror: Reflecting on Change
The Weeping Angels' Christmas Curse
Burrowed in Time: A Groundhog Day Journey
Heartbeats: Poems to Share with Your Valentine
Dino Wicca: The Sacred Grimoire of Prehistoric Magick
Courage of the Pride: Finding Your Inner Roar
The Lion's Leap: Bold Moves for Big Results
Healthy Hustle: Achieving Without Overworking
Practical Manifesting: Turning Dreams into Reality in 2025
Jurassic Pharaohs: Unlocking the Magick of Ancient Egypt and Dino Wicca
The Happiness Equation: Small Changes for Big Joy
The Confidence Compass: Finding Your Inner Strength
Whispers in the Hollow: Tales of the Forgotten Beasts
Echoes from the Hollow: The Return of Forgotten Beasts
The Hollow Ascendant: The Rise of the Forgotten Beasts
The Relationship Reset: Building Better Connections
Mastering the Morning: How to Win the Day Before 8 AM
The Shadow's Dance: Groundhog Day Symbolism
Cupid's Kitchen: Quick Valentine's Day Recipes
Valentine's Day on a Budget: Love Without Breaking the Bank
Astrocraft: Aligning the Stars in the World of Minecraft
Forecasting Life: Groundhog Day Reflections
Bleeding Hearts: Twisted Tales of Valentine's Terror
Herbal Smoke Revolution: The Ultimate Guide to Nature's Cigarette Alternative
Winter's Wrath: The Complete Survival Blueprint for Extreme Freezes.
The Groundhog's Shadow: A Tale of Seasons
Burrowed Insights: Wisdom from the Groundhog

Sensual Strings: The Art of Erotic Bondage
Whispered Flames: Unlocking the Power of Fire Play
Forgotten Shadows: A Guide to Cryptids Lost to Time
Six Weeks of Secrets: Groundhog Day's Hidden Messages
Shadows and Cycles: Groundhog Day Reflections
The Art of Love Letters: Crafting the Perfect Message
Romantic Getaways at Home: Turning Your Space into Paradise
Purrfect Brews: A Cat Lover's Guide to Coffee and Companionship
The Groundhog's Wisdom: Timeless Lessons for Modern Life
The Shadow Oracle: Groundhog Day as a Predictor
Emerging from the Burrow: A Journey of Renewal
The Language of Love: Learning Your Partner's Love Style
Authorpreneur: The Ultimate Blueprint for Writing, Publishing, and Thriving as an Author
Weathering the Seasons: Groundhog Day Perspectives
Valentine's Day Magic: A Guide to Romantic Rituals
The Shadow Chronicles: Stories of Groundhog Day
Love and Laughter: Fun Games for Valentine's Day
AstroRealty: Unlocking the Stars for Property Success
The Groundhog's Path: A Guide to Seasonal Balance
Groundhog Day Diaries: Reflections in the Shadow
The Groundhog's Light: Illuminating the Path Ahead
Valentine's Traditions from Around the World
AI Wealth Revolution: Unlocking the Trillionaire Mindset
Love Rekindled: Reigniting Passion in Relationships
Single and Thriving: Self-Love on Valentine's Day
Emerald Legends: Mystical Tales of Ireland
Green Alchemy: Harnessing Nature's Magic
The Hearts of Horror: A Valentine's Day Nightmare
The Leprechaun's Guide to Wealth and Wisdom
Dancing with the Sidhe: Celebrating the Otherworld

Shamrocks and Shadows: Mysteries of the Green Isle

Emerald Energy: Harnessing Luck and Growth

The Gingerbread Golem's Valentine: A Sweetheart's Guide to Love and Enchantment

The Celtic Knot: Weaving Life and Destiny

Green Fire: Elemental Magic for St. Patrick's Day

Clover Chronicles: Finding Your Inner Luck

Ireland's Mystical Creatures: A Field Guide

Gingerbread Golem's Love Almanac

Prowl and Thrive: The Lion's Guide to Success

Love Alchemy: Transforming Your Life Through Heart Energy

WORLD DOMINATION: Woman's Rule 3:The New Life

The Midnight Rose: A Guide to Lunar Love Spells

The Forbidden Letters: Writing Your Own Love Prophecy

Luck and Lore: St. Patrick's Day for Modern Mystics

The Green Path: A Pagan Celebration of Renewal

The Dark Architect's Guide to Reprogramming Reality

Prankster's Paradise: A Guide to Harmless Hijinks

Manifest Your Reality: The Law of Attraction Simplified

The TARDIS Owner's Manual: Understanding the Doctor's Ship: *A complete guide to the TARDIS, its technology, secrets, and mysteries*

Starlit Romance: Astrology Secrets for Finding True Love

The Time Lord's Atlas: A Complete Guide to the Whoniverse: ***A breakdown of the locations, planets, and dimensions explored in Doctor Who***

Sweetheart Shadows: The Dark Side of Love and Attraction

February Fire: Reigniting Passion in Every Area of Life

The Self-Love Toolkit: 5 Ways to Embrace Who You Are

February Sparks: Ignite Your Dreams in 28 Days

March to Success: A 31-Day Action Blueprint

Ancient Paths: The 13 Sacred Principles of Dino Wicca

Echoes of Tomorrow: Navigating the AI Revolution
The Wellness Blueprint: Balancing Mind, Body, and Soul
Green Horizons: Sustainable Living for a Better Tomorrow
The AI Wealth Code: How to Make Millions with Automation
AI-Powered Creativity: Writing, Art, and Music for Profit
Extinction Rites: Rebirthing Your Soul Through Prehistoric Magick
Sacred Serpents tarot
Celestial Enchantment blank journal
Star Strains
Culinary Journeys: Exploring Global Flavors at Home
The Hollowvale Curse
The Hollowvale Harvest
The Egg of Transformation: Awakening Your Inner Power
Blooming Into Power: A Wiccan Guide to Spring Awakening
The Nightmare Nexus: The Third Doctor's Perilous Haunting
Digital Detox: Reclaiming Your Life in a Connected World
Ostara's Path: Walking the Spiral of Renewal
The Sacred Hare
Financial Freedom: Building Wealth in the Modern Age
Spring's Cauldron: Stirring the Waters of Change
The Hollowvale Pact
Quantum Consciousness: The Science of Reality Shifting
The Hollowvale Hunger
The Sacred Waters Within: A Witch's Guide to Hydrocephalus Magick
The Raven's Nest: Building a Life of Unshakable Stability
AI and the Human Mind: The Future of Intelligence
The Hollowvale Reckoning
Timeless Love: Building and Maintaining Lasting Relationships
The Raven's Roar: Unlocking Unstoppable Confidence
Raven Sight: Awakening Intuition and Inner Wisdom

The Butterfly Effect: Small Changes, Big Transformations

Taming the Boogeyman: How to Conquer Your Inner Fears

The Magick of Green: Awakening Earth's Energy in You

The Entrepreneurial Mindset: Secrets to Business Success

The Hollowvale End

The Shadow Luck Ritual: Reclaiming Power from Your Dark Side

Spring Magick for Beginners: A Simple Guide to Seasonal Energy Work

Doctor Who: The Hollowvale Conundrum

The March of Miracles: Unlocking Synchronicities in Spring

Unveiling the Cosmos: A Guide to Stargazing and Space Exploration

The Ultimate Guide to Surviving an Economic Collapse

The AI Gold Rush: How to Profit from the AI Revolution

Bastet's Shadow: The Hidden Power of Feline Magick

The Bastet Codex: Unlocking the Goddess's Magickal Secrets

Purring Spells: Harnessing Bastet's Healing Frequencies

Bastet's Nine Lives: Rebirth, Transformation, and Immortality Spells

Primal Currents: Hydrocephalus Magick in the Path of Dino Wicca

The Digital Gold Rush: Mastering E-Commerce and Online Sales

Future Shock: Adapting to the Next Decade of Change

The Quantum Mindset: Think Like a Billionaire

Sacred Motherhood: Awakening the Divine Feminine Within

The Mother's Spellbook: Enchantments for Love, Protection, and Prosperity

The Witch's Guide to Parenting: Raising Empowered and Intuitive Children

The Magick of Motherhood: Reclaiming Your Power Through Rituals

The Pagan Path to Self-Love: A Goddess's Guide to Worth and Confidence
Wild Woman Magick: Unleashing Your Primal Power
The Money Magnet Blueprint: Unlocking Unlimited Wealth
Biohacking 101: Unlock Your Body's Full Potential
The Wild Father: A Pagan Guide to Strength and Wisdom
The Sacred Masculine: Unlocking Your Inner Power
The Druid's Compass
The Warrior's Mindset
The Father's Fire
Odin's Path
Ancestral Bonds
The House That Whispers
The Magician's Code
The Wild Hunt
The Green Man's Path
The Altar of Success
The Shadow and the Sword
The High Priestess's Guide to Energy Healing
The Lunar Mother
The Sacred Self-Care Grimoire
The Womb Wisdom Codex
The Wheel of the Mother
The Witch's Guide to Manifestation
The Q2 Reset
The Ultimate Guide to AI-Powered Passive Income
Escape the 9-5
AI Feline Fortunes
The Tear-Stained Grimoire
Razorblade Runes
Cemetery Sirens
The Midnight Wristwatch
The Town That Forgets

AI Horror & Creepypasta
The Hollow Frequency
The Breach Echo
The Quiet Between Worlds
The Sigil of Tharan-Khul
Summon the Vault of Y'ha'ten
The Becoming Codex
The Profit of Az'ra-nar
The Drowned Logos
Echoes of the Eldritch Will
The Deep Ledger
Necronomicon of Networth
Covenant of the Wealthwyrm
The Whisperer's Manifesto
The Rites of Azh-K'luth
The Ark of the Crawling Coin
The Tithe of Shadows
Inkheart Abyss
The Timewinds of Y'ha-nthlei
The Spiral Labyrinth of Azag-Nirrh
The Gallifreyan Heresy of the Black Pharaoh
The Psalms of Nyog-Sotha
Black Rain Alchemy
The Infinite Maw
The Entropic Blueprint
The Oracle of Sh'guul
The Book of Breach
The Drowned Saint's Testament
Dreamcraft of the Sleeper God
The Silence Market
Cthonomics: The Dark Wealth Algorithm
Invocation of the Ten-Eyed King
Wealthbound to the Wyrm Below

Become the Unnameable
Codex of the Sovereign Flame
Rituals of Relentless Becoming
The Shadow Ascends
The Eyes Beneath You
The Will That Wakes Worlds
Silence Is a Weapon
The Mirror That Screams
The Whisper Between Moments
The Mind That Devours Fear
The Myth of the Finished Self
The Architect of Your Madness
The Voice You've Buried
The Discipline of Madness
Stormborn: Awakening Your Inner Tempest
The Mind That Ate Time
Unbind Your Becoming
The Pact You Owe Yourself
The Devourer's Diet
The Acid That Carves the Path
The Tower You Must Burn
The Breath Between Worlds
Speak Like the Deep
The Labyrinth Within
The Spine of the Sea God
Rejection Is a Portal
The Crown You Refused
The Scar Is the Spell
The Lightless Flame
The Habit of Becoming Horrific
ChickenJockey Chaos
The Gatekeeper Within
You Are Not Your Name

The Compass of the Mad
The Archive of Unsent Letters
What the Mirror Can't Show You
The Knife You Needed
Worship Nothing, Become Everything
The Other Voice
The Body the World Forgot
The Vein of the Void
The Black Bone Codex
The Puzzle of the Hidden Self (Millennium Puzzle)
The Eye That Sees the Lie *(Millennium Eye)*
The Ring of Return (Millennium Ring)
The Rod of Relentless Will *(Millennium Rod)*
The Tally of the Soul (Millennium Tauk/Necklace)
The Key to the Locked Timeline (Millennium Key)
The Scale of Sacred Decisions (Millennium Scales)
Inferno Bites: The UnOfficial Minecraft Lava Cookbook
Rot in the Attic
Prana: The Hidden Force of Your Infinite Self
The Shadow Realm Within: Transforming Darkness Into Destiny
The Borderland Collapse
Claws of Protection: Bastet's Defensive Magick
Mr. Ring-a-Ding's Madness
Yugioh Astrology: Celestial Deckcraft and Duel Destiny (2026–2027 Edition)
The Seal You Signed: Unlocking the Power You Once Feared
The Puzzle of Infinite Minds: Unlocking the Mentalism Hidden Within
The Eye That Mirrors the All: Secrets of Inner Reflection
Doctor Who: The Toymaker's Broadcast
The Rod of Eternal Flow: Commanding the Currents of Vibration

Golden Eyes of Bastet: Enhancing Psychic Vision
The Key of Dual Forces: Balance Within the Polarity
The Scales of Living Rhythm: Timing the Dance of Life
The Necklace of Hidden Cause: Weaving the Webs of Fate
The Ring of Secret Masters: Rising Through the All Within All
Daggers of the Dying Deep
Bastet's Wealth and Fortune Magick: Prosperity Rituals of the Goddess
The Tide that Speaks
The Scrolls of Petosiris: 13 Rituals from the Feathered Eye
Petosiris and the Living Plague of Osirion
Feline Fire: Bastet's Passion and Love Magick
The Star Altar of Petosiris
Bastet's Whiskers: Supernatural Sensory Magick
The Bastet Grimoire
Feeding the Shadows
The Mouthless Prayer
The Spiral Wound
Becoming the Ibis: Lessons from Petosiris's Mind
The Crimson Coven: Cola Magick for Sweet Dominion
Sacred Cat's Paw
The Soda Zodiac: A Flavor for Every Sign
Covenant of the Crawling Flame
The Ink of Ish'Zur
Frothroot: The Thirst That Ate the World
The Golden Glyphs of Prosperity
The Etherbind Codex
Echoes of the Resistance: Reclaiming the You That Survived
Harnessed Minds: Breaking Free from Mental Control
The Eyes in the Smoke
Rootwake: The Carbon Covenant
Skitter Logic: Unlearning the Fear That Built You

Doctor Who: The World That Froths
Rootwake: The Fizz That Rewrites Flesh
Rootwake: Frothfather of the World
The Holly Pact: Blood Beneath the Mistletoe
The 2nd Mass Principle: Building Unbreakable Tribes
Web of Wits: A Survival Guide to Encounters with Anasi the Spider (Aunt Nancy)
The Hexbreaking Handbook: Effective Spells to Remove Curses
Pop Alchemy: Transform Your Life One Sip at a Time
The Mason Code: Leading in Unleadable Times
Petosiris and the Fifth Chamber of Thoth
The Ether Seed Within
The Parent of Tomorrow
Petosiris's Pyramid of Perpetual Wealth
Unlearn the World
Grimoire of the Hollow Tongue
Zodiac Weeds: Finding Your Strain Through the Stars
Aquarius Rises in the Bank
The Sugar God's Smile
The Skinclock Reversal: Biohacking the Face of Time
Debtburn: How to Obliterate What You Owe Forever
The Ice Cream Oracle: What Your Cone Says About Your Future
Silence Is Sovereignty: The Power of Being Unreadable
The Wind That Whispers Through Stone
Path of the Four Directions
Doctor Who: The Maestro's Symphony of Endings
Oxygen Grail: Breathing to Undo the Clock
Zodiacal Collapse: When Stars Devour Time
Teachings from the Red Sand Silence
Doctor Who: Omega – The Broken Equation
Memory Wipe Your Past: Start Over Like a MiB

Mitochondria Prime: Ignite the Core of Youth

A Nest of Roaches

Grub from the Galaxy: MiB Recipes You'll Never Forget

Whiskers of Power: Bastet's Guide to Inner Sovereignty

The Gift Must Cost Them: Negotiation Through Unequal Exchange

The Worm Guys' Wealth Code: Hustle Like an Alien

Bug Out: The Edgar Method for Ruthless Goal Setting

Weaving Life with Spiderwoman's Pattern

Doctor Who: The Rani's Renaissance

How to Get a Job (If You're a Puppygirl)

Speak Through Others: The Art of Proxy Power

T-Rex Your Trauma: Reclaim the Power of Your Primal Self

The Black Briefcase: How MiB Stay Wealthy in Silence

The Thirst Beyond Reason: Understanding Diabetes Insipidus From the Inside Out

Backwoods Witchcraft for Billionaires: The Pagan Path from Dirt Roads to Gold Roads

The Moonshine Grimoire: Fermented Spells for Abundance

The Nameless Geometry

The Wraith's Mixtape: Spellcasting with Songs of Sorrow

The Gallifreyan Gentleman: Silent Wealth, Sonic Confidence, and the Doctor's Code of Living

Sugar Water Confidence

Dino Totems: Spirit Guides from Earth's First Gods

Pumpkin Sigils & Ritual Smoke

The Hózhó Compass

The Distortus Discipline – Order from Inner Mutation

Witchcraft for the Cold-Blooded Soul

Moonlight Over the Blessingway

Water, Interrupted: When the Body Forgets How to Hold On

Deformed but Divine: Embracing Your Asymmetry

Hexes in the Henhouse: The Farm Witch's Guide to Power

The Reversed Flame: A Grimoire of Inverted Power

Salt, Cells, and Sanity: Reclaiming Balance with Diabetes Insipidus

King of the Broken: Crowning the Flawed Self

Moonlight Scars: Emo Moon Magick and the Art of Lunar Sorrow

Noose Spells: Magick of the Hanging Rope

The Goth Cathedral: Rituals of the Broken and Beautiful

The Cretaceous Codex: Dino Spirits and Fossil Magick

The Turkey Bones Ritual

Nine Lives of Manifestation: Unlocking Bastet's Reality Codes

Chaos Muscles: Building Strength from Twisted Pain

Emo Blood Magick: The Veins of Power

The 3AM Flood: Nighttime Urination, Sleep Loss, and the DI Spiral

The Silence Between the Stars

The Lemon Method: Sour Your Way to Success

Starlit Sovereign

The Rite of Twelve Gates: Walking the Gates of the Duat.

Cornbread and Conjure: Recipes for Riches and Rootwork

The Black Rose Rituals: Emo Love Spells and Obsession Magick

The Eternal Goodbye: Death Magick and Rebirth Rituals

Sinkrot: The Drain That Remembers

The Hybrid Mindset: Thinking Beyond Evolution

Bone Dry: Navigating Dehydration Before It Breaks You

Wreathcraft: Winter Sigils and Yuletide Spells

The Rite of Twelve Mouths

S'mores of the Damned: Haunted Recipes for Halloween Night

Rethink the Drink: A Beverage Survival Guide for DI Warriors

The Shadow Chord: Guitar Magick and Sonic

Malformed Yet Majestic: Leading When You Feel Wrong Inside

The Cursed Diary: Ink-Stained Spells of the Emo Soul

Anxiety Off Switch: Emergency Reset for a Fried Nervous System

The Energy Heist: How to Take Back Your Life from Drainers

Beyond the Bathroom: Rebuilding Your Social Life With DI

Coyote's Gift for Decision Makers

Ghoul-Goo: Spooky S'mores You'll Die For

Echoes in the Mirror: Scrying and Self-Destruction Magick

Thread and Thorn: Stitching Spells from Rural Cloth

The Mogwai Mind: Building Untouchable Wealth from Small Ideas

Be Your Own Guide: Trust Your Inner Compass

Hormones in Chaos: The Endocrine Puzzle of Diabetes Insipidus

ChronoCleanse: Detox Your Biological Timeline

The Limb You Hide Is the One That Saves You

Leaves, Bones, and Whisper Spells

The Dinosaur Mindset: Prehistoric Tactics for Modern Wealth

Clawing Back Control: A Bastet Method for Boundaries and Empowerment

Samhain Codes of the Forgotten

Orange Alchemy: The Autumnal Spellbook

Monster Within, Master Without

The Sigil That Sleeps

Hearthcraft: Yule Hearth Sigils and Winter Warmth Spells

Temple of the Purring Moon: Rituals from Bastet's Lineage

When the Earth Remembers Your Footsteps

Food for Mood: Eat to Heal Depression, Not Just Survive It

Witch of the Kudzu Vine: Southern Pagan Wealth Secrets

The Invisible Diagnosis: Advocating for Yourself With DI

The Coffin's Lullaby: Sleep Magick and Nightmares as Portals

Ashes of the Will: Rituals for Erasing the Self

The Fracture Rite: Shattering the Magickal Core

Funeral Candles: The Art of Emo Flame Magick

The Black Grimoire: A Blank Ritual for Writing in Absence

Phantom Thirst: A Halloween Survival Guide for Diabetes Insipidus

The Hollow Crown: Emo Royalty and Magick of the Outcast King

Sandpainting for the Soul

Falling Into Balance: Using the Extra Hour to Recalibrate Life

100 Southern Superstitions That Still Work

The DI Child: A Parent's Guide to Raising Hydrated, Happy Kids

The Jungle of Shame: Escaping the Hidden Lab of Doubt

The Witch's Toast: S'mores Spells and Creepy Confections

The Hoodoo Pantry: Spells from the Mason Jar

The Immortal Fortune: Secret Wealth Lessons from Captain Jack Harkness

The Specter's Embrace: Magick for Channeling Ghostly Lovers

Grateful Waters: A Thanksgiving Survival Guide for Diabetes Insipidus

The Seizure Gospel

Harvestbind: Autumn Sigils and Samhain Spells

Doctor Who: The Algorithmic Awakening

Silent Nights, Steady Waters: A Christmas Survival Guide for Diabetes Insipidus

The Extra Hour Effect: How One Hour Can Transform Everything

Blade Between the Breaths

Running with the Mountain Shadows

Echoes of the Failed Experiment – Becoming a Living Legacy

Swamp Witches & River Ghosts: Real Southern Hauntings

Cornbread Prophecies: Magical Recipes from a Southern Table

Doctor Who: The Signal in the Star

Bloomcraft: Spring Sigils and Equinox Enchantments

Get Some Tarot cards: https://www.makeplayingcards.com/sell/apophis-occult-shop

Get some shirts: https://www.bonfire.com/store/apophis-shirt-emporium/

Instagrams:
@apophis_enterprises,
@apophisbookemporium,
@apophisscardshop
Twitter: @apophisenterpr1
Tiktok:@apophisenterprise
Youtube: @sg1fan23477
Hive: @sg1fan23477
CheeLee: @SG1fan23477

Podcast: Apophis Chat Zone: https://open.spotify.com/show/5zXbrCLEV2xzCp8ybrfHsk?si=fb4d4fdbdce44dec

Newsletter: https://apophiss-newsletter-27c897.beehiiv.com/

If you want to support me or see posts of other projects that I have come over to: **buymeacoffee.com/mpetchinskg**

I post there daily several times a day

Get your Dinowicca or Christmas themed digital products, especially Santa Raptor songs and other musics. Here: **https://sg1fan23477.gumroad.com**

Apophis Yuletide Digital has not only digital Christmas items, but it will have all things with Dinowicca as well as other Digital products.

www.ingramcontent.com/pod-product-compliance
Lightning Source LLC
LaVergne TN
LVHW022225200926
848481LV00006B/2116